Stories of Success:

Slow and Sure
(Illustrated)

Stories of Success:

Slow and Sure
(Illustrated)

Horatio Alger, Jr.

Sumner Books
Hermosa Beach, CA

TABLE OF CONTENTS

A NOTE FROM THE PUBLISHER

Once crowned "America's most influential writer," Horatio Alger is hardly known today. Those who are familiar with him think "rags to riches," and that's about it. Most young people have never heard of him.

What an opportunity!

More than a hundred years before our contemporary self-help movement, Horatio Alger paved the way with his vivid illustrations of the keys to success and happiness. Today, Sumner Books is excited to introduce a new generation of Americans to some of the most inspirational stories ever written. Regardless of your age, you simply cannot read a Horatio Alger book without coming away with a good feeling.

Alger's books initially sold in the millions and then the tens of millions and finally the hundreds of millions. In fact, the Chicago Daily News once called Horatio Alger "America's best-selling author of all time." Sumner Books is committed to bringing to life this best-selling collection in the form of audiobooks read by professional actors and recorded with audio engineers in our studio. Our revised e-books, each with a detailed table of contents and colored illustrations, are professionally edited, including the occasional updating of phrases to make the books as easy to read today as they were when they were first published between 1865 and 1900.

Long after his death in 1899, the magazine Publishers Weekly wrote: "To call Horatio Alger Jr. America's most influential writer may seem like an overstatement ... but ... only Benjamin Franklin meant as much to the formation of the American popular mind."

Our goal is to bring back some of the influence that Alger exerted on millions of young people in America. Yes, it's retro; it's counterintuitive and totally contrary to the cynicism that has become a part of American culture. But we are proud to be leading a movement that is as positive and uplifting as the last pages of a Horatio Alger story.

Rick Newcombe
President
Sumner Books

Stories of Success

"No legacy is so rich as honesty."
William Shakespeare

CHAPTER I

SIX MONTHS AFTER

"It's almost time for Paul to come home," said Mrs. Hoffman. "I must be setting the table for dinner."

"I wonder how he will like my new picture," said Jimmy, a delicate boy of eight, whose refined features, thoughtful look, and high brow showed that his mind by no means shared the weakness of his body. Though only eight years of age he already manifested a remarkable taste and talent for drawing, in which he had acquired surprising skill, considering that he had never taken lessons, but had learned all he knew from copying such pictures as fell in his way.

"Let me see your picture, Jimmy," said Mrs. Hoffman. "Have you finished it?"

She came up and looked over his shoulder. He had been engaged in copying a humorous picture from the last page of Harper's Weekly. It was an ambitious attempt on the part of so young a pupil, but he had succeeded remarkably well, reproducing with close fidelity the grotesque expressions of the figures introduced in the picture.

"That is excellent, Jimmy," said his mother in warm commendation.

The little boy looked gratified.

"Do you think I will be an artist some day?" he asked.

"I have no doubt of it," said his mother, "if you can only obtain suitable instruction. However, there is plenty of time for that. You are only seven years old."

"I shall be eight tomorrow," said Jimmy, straightening up his slender form with the pride which every boy feels in advancing age.

"So you will. I had forgotten it."

"I wonder whether I can earn as much money as Paul when I get as old," said Jimmy thoughtfully. "I don't think I can. I shan't be half as strong."

"It isn't always the strongest who earn the most money," said his mother.

"But Paul is smart as well as strong."

"So are you smart. You can read unusually well for a boy of your age, and in drawing I think Paul is hardly your equal, though he is twice as old."

—

Jimmy laughed.

"That's true, mother," he said. "Paul tried to draw a horse the other day, and it looked more like a cow."

"You see then that we all have our different gifts. Paul has a talent for business."

"I think he'll be rich some day, mother."

"I hope he will, for I think he will make a good use of his money."

While Mrs. Hoffman was speaking she had been setting the table for dinner. The meal was not a luxurious one, but there was no lack of food. Beside rolls and butter, there was a plate of cold meat, an apple pie, and a pot of steaming hot tea. The cloth was scrupulously clean, and I am sure that though the room was a humble one not one of my readers need have felt a repugnance to sitting down at Mrs. Hoffman's plain table.

For the benefit of such as may not have read "Paul the Peddler," I will explain briefly that Mrs. Hoffman, by the death of her husband two years previous, had been reduced to poverty, which compelled her to move into a tenement house and live as best she could on the earnings of her oldest son, Paul, supplemented by the pittance she obtained for sewing. Paul, a smart, enterprising boy, after trying most of the street occupations, had become a young street merchant. By a lucky chance he had obtained capital enough to buy out a necktie stand below the Astor House, where his tact and energy had enabled him to achieve a success, the details of which we will presently give. Besides his own profits, he was able to employ his mother in making neckties at a compensation considerably greater than she could have obtained from the Broadway shops for which she had hitherto worked.

Scarcely was dinner placed on the table when Paul entered. He was a stout, manly boy of fifteen, who would readily have been taken for a year or two older, with a frank, handsome face, and an air of confidence and self-reliance, which he had acquired through his independent efforts to gain a livelihood. He had been thrown upon his own resources at an age when most boys have everything done for them, and though this had been a disadvantage so far as his education was concerned, it had developed in him a confidence in himself and his own ability to cope with the world not usually found in boys of his age.

4

"Well, mother," said he briskly, "I am glad dinner is ready, for I am as hungry as a wolf."

"I think there will be enough for you," said his mother, smiling. "If not, we will send to the baker's for an extra supply."

"Is a wolf hungry, Paul?" asked Jimmy, soberly accepting Paul's simile.

"I'll draw you one after supper, Jimmy, and you can judge," answered Paul.

"Your animals all look like cows, Paul," said his little brother.

"I see you are jealous of me," said Paul, with much indignation, "because I draw better than you."

"After supper you can look at my last picture," said Jimmy. "It is copied from Harper's Weekly."

"Pass it along now, Jimmy. I don't think it will spoil my appetite."

Jimmy handed it to his brother with a look of pardonable pride.

"Excellent, Jimmy. I couldn't do it better myself," said Paul. "You are a little genius."

"I like drawing so much, Paul. I hope some time I can do something else besides copy."

"No doubt you will. I am sure you will be a famous artist some day, and make no end of money by your pictures."

"That's what I would like—to make money."

"Fie, Jimmy! I had no idea you were so fond of money."

"I would like to help mother just as you are doing, Paul. Do you think I will ever earn as much as you do?"

"A great deal more, I hope, Jimmy. Nevertheless, I am doing well," added Paul in a tone of satisfaction. "Did you know, mother, it is six months today since I bought out the necktie stand?"

"Is it, Paul?" asked his mother with interest. "Have you succeeded as well as you anticipated?"

"Better, mother. It was a good idea putting in a case of knives. They help along my profits. Why, I sold four knives today, making on an average twenty-five cents each."

"Did you? That is indeed worthwhile."

"It is more than I used to average for a whole day's earnings before I went into this business."

"How many neckties did you sell, Paul?" asked Jimmy.

"I sold fourteen."

"How much profit did you make on each?"

"About fourteen cents. Can you tell how much that makes?"

"I could cipher it out on my slate."

"No matter; I'll tell you. It makes a dollar and ninety-six cents. That, added to the money I made on the knives, amounts to two dollars and ninety-six cents."

"Almost three dollars."

"Yes; sometimes I sell more neckties, but then I don't always sell as many knives. However, I am satisfied."

"I have made two dozen neckties today, Paul," said his mother.

"I am afraid you did too much, mother."

"Oh, no. There isn't much work about a necktie."

"Then I owe you a dollar and twenty cents, mother."

"I don't think you ought to pay me five cents apiece, Paul."

"That's fair enough, mother. If I get fourteen cents for selling a tie, certainly you ought to get five cents for making one."

"But your money goes to support us, Paul."

"And where does yours go, mother?"

"A part of it has gone for a new dress, Paul. I went up to Stewart's today and bought a dress pattern. I will show it to you after dinner."

"That's right, mother. You don't buy enough new dresses. Considering that you are the mother of a successful merchant, you ought to dash out. Doesn't Jimmy want some clothes?"

"I am going to buy him a new suit tomorrow. He is eight years old tomorrow."

"Is he? What an old fellow you are getting to be, Jimmy! How many gray hairs have you got?"

"I haven't counted," said Jimmy, laughing.

"I tell you what, mother, we must celebrate Jimmy's birthday. He is the only artist in the family, and we must treat him with proper consideration. I'll tell you what, Jimmy, I'll close up my business at twelve o'clock, and give all my clerks a half-holiday. Then I'll take you and mother to Barnum's Museum, where you can see all the curiosities, and the play besides. How would you like that?"

"Ever so much, Paul," said the little boy, his eyes brightening at the prospect. "There's a giant there, isn't there? How tall is he?"

"Somewhere about eighteen feet, I believe."

"Now you are making fun, Paul."

"Well, it's either eighteen or eight, one or the other. Then there's a dwarf, two feet high, or is it inches?"

—

"Of course it's feet. He couldn't be so little as two inches."

"Well, Jimmy, I dare say you're right. Then it's settled that we go to the museum tomorrow. You must go with us, mother."

"Oh, yes, I will go," said Mrs. Hoffman, "and I presume I shall enjoy it nearly as much as Jimmy."

CHAPTER II

BARNUM'S MUSEUM

Barnum's Museum now lives only in the past. Its successor, known as Wood's Museum, is situated at the corner of Twenty-ninth Street and Broadway. But at the time of my story the old Barnum's stood below the Astor House, on the site now occupied by those magnificent structures, the Herald building and the Park Bank. Here flowed daily and nightly a crowd of visitors who certainly got the worth of their money, only twenty-five cents, in the numberless varied curiosities which the unequaled showman had gathered from all quarters of the world.

THE FIRST BARNUM'S MUSEUM, New York.

Barnum's Museum, where they take Jimmy for his birthday.

Jimmy had often seen the handbills and advertisements of the museum, but had never visited it, and now anticipated with eagerness the moment when all its wonders should be revealed to him. In fact, he woke up about two hours earlier than usual to think of the treat in store for him.

Paul, as he had promised, closed up his business at twelve o'clock and came home. At half-past one the three were on their way to the museum. The distance was but short, and a very few minutes found them in the museum. Jimmy's eyes opened wide as they took in the crowded exhibition room, and he hardly knew what to look at first, until the approach of a giant eight feet high irresistibly attracted

---

8

him. It is a remarkable circumstance that Barnum's giants were always eight feet high on the bill, though not always by measure. Sometimes the great showman lavishly provided two or three of these Titans. Where they came from nobody knew. It has been conjectured by some that they were got up to order; but upon this point I cannot speak with certainty. As a general thing they are good-natured and harmless, in spite of their formidable proportions, and ready to have a joke at their own expense.

Edward Beupre . One of P.T. Barnum's giants.

"Oh, see that big man!" exclaimed Jimmy, struck with awe, as he surveyed the formidable proportions of the giant.

"He's bigger than you will ever be, Jimmy," said Paul.

"I wouldn't like to be so tall," said the little boy.

"Why not? You could whip all the fellows that tried to tease you."

"They don't tease me much, Paul."

"Do they tease you at all?" asked his brother quickly.

"Not very often. Sometimes they call me Limpy, because I am lame."

"I'd like to catch any boy doing it," said Paul energetically. "I'd make him see stars."

"I don't mind, Paul."

"But I do. Just let me catch the next fellow that calls you Limpy, and he won't do it again."

By this time a group had gathered round the giant. Paul and Jimmy joined it.

"Was you always so large?" asked a boy at Paul's side.

"I was rather smaller when I was a baby," said the giant, laughing.

"How much do you weigh?"

"Two hundred and seventy-five pounds."

"That beats you, Jimmy," said Paul.

"Were you big when you were a boy?"

"I was over seven feet high on my fifteenth birthday," said the giant.

"Did the teacher lick you often?" asked one of the boys shyly.

"Not very often. He couldn't take me over his knee very well."

"What an awful lot of cloth you must take for your clothes!" said the last boy.

"That's so, my lad. I keep a manufactory running all the time to keep me supplied."

"Do you think that's true, Paul?" asked Jimmy, doubtfully.

"Not quite," answered Paul, smiling.

"Don't you need to eat a good deal?" was the next question.

"Oh, no, not much. Half a dozen chickens and a couple of turkeys are about all I generally eat for lunch. Perhaps I could eat more if I tried. If any of you boys will invite me to lunch I'll do my best."

"I'm glad you ain't my son," said one of the boys. "I shouldn't like to keep you in food and clothes."

"Well, now, I shouldn't mind having you for a father," said the giant, humorously looking down upon his questioner, a boy of twelve, and rather small of his age, with a humorous twinkle in his eye. "You wouldn't whip me very often, would you?"

Here there was a laugh at the expense of the small boy, and the group dispersed.

"Now, you've seen a large man, Jimmy," said Paul. "I'm going next to show you a small one."

They moved on to a different part of the building, and joined another crowd, this time surrounding the illustrious Tom Thumb, at that time one of the attractions of the museum.

Tom Thumb. One of the people working at Barnum's Museum.

"There's a little man, smaller than you are, Jimmy," said Paul.

"So he is," said Jimmy. "Is that Tom Thumb?"

"Yes."

"I didn't think he was so small. I'm glad I'm not so little."

"No, it might not be very comfortable, though you could make a good deal of money by it. Tom is said to be worth over a hundred thousand dollars."

"I guess it doesn't cost him so much for clothes as the giant."

"Probably not. I don't think he would need to run a manufactory for his own use."

But there were multitudes of curiosities to be seen, and they could not linger long. Jimmy was particularly interested in the waxwork figures, which at first he thought must be real, so natural was their appearance. There were lions and tigers in cages, who looked out from between the gratings as if they would like nothing better than to make a hearty meal from one or more of the crowd who surrounded the cages. Jimmy clung to Paul's hand timidly.

"Couldn't they get out, Paul?" he asked.

"No, the cages are too strong. But even if they could, I don't think they would attack you. You would only be a mouthful for them."

"I don't see how Mr. Barnum dared to put them in the cages."

"I don't think Barnum would dare to come very near them. But he has keepers who are used to them."

But it was time for the afternoon performance to commence. The play was Uncle Tom's Cabin, which no doubt many of my readers have seen. They got very good seats, fronting the stage, though some distance back. When the curtain rose Jimmy's attention was at once absorbed. It was the first time he had ever seen a play, and it seemed to him a scene of rare enchantment. To Paul, however, it was much less of a novelty. He had frequently been to Barnum's and the Old Bowery, though not as often as those boys who had no home in which to spend their evenings. Mrs. Hoffman was scarcely less interested than Jimmy in the various scenes of the play. It was not particularly well acted, for most of the actors were indifferent in point of talent; but then none of the three were critics, and could not have told the difference between them and first-class performers.

Both laughed heartily over the eccentricities of Topsy, probably the most original character in Mrs. Stowe's popular story, and Jimmy was affected to tears at the death of little Eva. To his unaccustomed eyes it seemed real, and he felt as if Eva was really dying. But, taking it altogether, it was an afternoon of great enjoyment to Jimmy, whose pleasures were not many.

"Well, Jimmy, how did you like it?" asked Paul, as they were working their way out slowly through the crowd.

"It was beautiful, Paul. I am so much obliged to you for taking me."

"I am glad you liked it, Jimmy. We will go again some time."

They were stepping out on the sidewalk, when a boy about Paul's size jostled them rudely.

"There's Limpy!" said he, with a rude laugh.

"You'd better not say that again, Peter Blake," he said menacingly.

"Why not?" demanded Peter defiantly.

"It won't be safe," said Paul significantly.

"I'll call you Limpy if I like."

"You may call me so, and I won't mind it. But don't you call my little brother names."

"I don't mind, Paul," said Jimmy.

"But I do," said Paul. "No boy shall call you names when I am near."

Paul's resolute character was well understood by all the boys who knew him, and Peter would not have ventured to speak as he did, but he did not at first perceive that Jimmy was accompanied by his brother. When he did discover it he slunk away as soon as he could.

They were walking up Park Row, when Jim Parker, once an enemy, but now a friend of Paul, met them. He looked excited, and hurried up to meet them.

"When were you home, Paul?" he asked abruptly.

"Two or three hours ago. I have just come from Barnum's."

"Then you don't know what's happened?"

Paul turned instantly.

"No. What is it?"

"Your house has caught fire, and is burning down. The engines are there, but I don't think they can save it."

"Let us hurry home, brother," said Paul. "It's lucky I've got my bank-book with me, so if we are burned out, we can get another home at once."

Excited by this startling intelligence, they quickened their steps, and soon stood in front of the burning building.

CHAPTER III

THE BURNING OF THE

TENEMENT HOUSE

The scene was an exciting one. The occupants of the large tenement house had vacated their rooms in alarm, each bearing what first came to hand, and reinforced by a numerous crowd of outsiders, were gazing in dismay at the sudden conflagration which threatened to make them homeless.

"Och hone! och hone! that iver I should see the day!" exclaimed a poor Irish woman, wringing her hands. "It's ruined intirely I am by the fire. Is that you, Mrs. Hoffman, and Paul? Indade it's a sad day for the likes of us."

"It is indeed, Mrs. McGowan. Do you know how the fire caught?"

"It's all along of that drunken brute, Jim O'Connel. He was smokin' in bed, bad luck to him, as drunk as a baste, and the burnin' tobacker fell out on the shates, and set the bed on fire."

"Cheer up, Mrs. McGowan!" said the hearty voice of Mrs. Donovan. "We ain't burnt up ourselves, and that's a comfort."

"I've lost all my money," said Mrs. McGowan disconsolately. "I had twenty-siven dollars and thirty cents in the bank, and the bank-book's burnt up, och hone!"

"You can get your money for all that, Mrs. McGowan," said Paul. "Just tell them at the savings-bank how you lost your book, and they will give you another."

"Do you think so?" asked Mrs. McGowan doubtfully.

"I feel sure of it."

"Then that's something," said she, looking considerably relieved. "Whin can I get it?"

"I will go with you to the bank tomorrow."

"Thank you, Paul. And it's you that's a fine lad intirely."

"All my pictures will burn up," said Jimmy.

"You can draw some new ones," said Paul. "I am afraid, mother, you will never wear that new dress of yours."

"It's a pity I bought it just at this time."

"Here's a bundle I took from your room, Mrs. Hoffman," said a boy, pushing his way through the crowd.

"My dress is safe after all," said Mrs. Hoffman in surprise. "It is the only thing we shall save."

"You can have it made up and wear it in remembrance of the fire, mother."

"I shall be likely to remember that without."

Meanwhile the fire department was working energetically to put out the fire. Stream after stream was directed against the burning building, but the fire had gained too great headway. It kept on its victorious course, triumphantly baffling all the attempts that were made to extinguish it. Then efforts were made to prevent its spreading to the neighboring buildings, and these were successful. But the building itself, old and rotten, a very tinderbox, was doomed. In less than an hour the great building, full as a hive of occupants, was a confused mass of smoking ruins. And still the poor people hovered around in uncertainty and dismay, in that peculiarly forlorn condition of mind induced by the thought that they knew not where they should lay their heads during the coming night. One family had saved only a teakettle to commence their housekeeping with. A little girl had pressed close to her breast a shapeless and dirty rag baby, her most valued possession. A boy of twelve had saved a well-used pair of skates, for which he had traded the day before, while an old woman, blear-eyed and wrinkled, hobbled about, groaning, holding in one hand a looking-glass, an article the most unlikely of all, one would think, to be of use to her.

"Did you save nothing, Mrs. Donovan?" asked Paul.

"Shure and I saved my flatirons, and my tub I threw out of the window, but some spalpeen has walked off with it. I wish it had fallen on his head. What'll my Pat say when he comes home from work?"

"It's lucky no lives were lost."

"Thrue for you, Mrs. Hoffman. It might have been a dale worse. I don't mind meself, for I've strong arms, and I'll soon be on my fate again. But my Pat'll be ravin'. He had just bought a new coat to go to a ball wid tomorrow night, and it's all burnt up in the fire. Do you see that poor craythur wid the lookin' glass? I'm glad I didn't save mine, for I wouldn't know what to do wid it."

"Well, Mrs. Donovan, we must find a new home."

"I've got a sister livin' on Mulberry Street. She'll take me in till I can get time to turn round. But I must stay here till my Pat comes home, or he would think I was burnt up too."

The crowd gradually diminished. Every family, however poor, had some relations or acquaintances who were willing to give them a temporary shelter, though in most cases it fed to most uncomfortable crowding. But the poor know how to sympathize with the poor, and cheerfully bore the discomfort for the sake of alleviating the misfortune which might some day come upon themselves.

"Where shall we go, mother?" asked Jimmy anxiously.

Mrs. Hoffman looked doubtfully at Paul.

"I suppose we must seek shelter somewhere," she said.

"How will the Fifth Avenue Hotel suit you?" asked Paul.

"I think I will wait till my new dress is finished," she said, smiling faintly.

"Why, what's the matter, Paul? You're not burnt out, are you?"

Turning at the voice, Paul recognized Sam Norton, a newsboy, who sold papers near his own stand.

"Just about so, Sam," he answered. "We're turned into the street."

"And where are you going to stop overnight?"

"That's more than I know. Mother here isn't sure whether she prefers the St. Nicholas or Fifth Avenue."

"Paul likes to joke at my expense," said Mrs. Hoffman.

"Come over and stop with us tonight," said Sam. "My mother'll be glad to have you."

"Thank you, Sam," said Mrs. Hoffman, who knew the boy as a friend of Paul, "but I shouldn't like to trouble your mother."

"It'll be no trouble," said Sam eagerly.

"If you think it won't, Sam," said Paul, "we'll accept for tonight. I am afraid they wouldn't take us in at any of the big hotels with only one dress, and that not made up, by way of baggage. Tomorrow I'll find some other rooms."

"Come along, then," said Sam, leading the way. "We'll have a jolly time tonight, Paul."

"By way of celebrating the fire. It's jolly enough for us, but I shouldn't like it too often."

"I say, Paul," said Sam, wheeling round, "if you're out of stamps, I've got a dollar or two that I can spare."

"Thank you, Sam; you're a brick! But I've saved my bank-book, and I've got plenty to start on. Much obliged to you, all the same."

It was true that Paul was in an unusually good position to withstand the blow which had so unexpectedly fallen upon him. He had a hundred and fifty dollars in the hands of Mr. Preston, a wealthy gentleman who took an interest in him, and moreover had a hundred dollars deposited to his credit in a savings-bank, besides his stock in trade, probably amounting to at least fifty dollars, at the wholesale price. So there was no immediate reason for anxiety. It would have been rather awkward, however, to look up a shelter for the night at such short notice, and therefore Sam Norton's invitation was particularly welcome.

Sam led the way to the lodgings occupied by his parents. They were located on Pearl Street, not far from Centre, and were more spacious and well furnished than any in the burned tenement house.

"You go up first and tell your mother, Sam," said Paul. "She won't know what to make of it if we go in without giving her any notice."

"All right," said Sam. "I'll be down in a jiffy."

Two minutes were sufficient for Sam to explain the situation. His mother, a good, motherly woman, at once acknowledged the claim upon her hospitality. She came downstairs at once, and said heartily to Paul, whom she knew:

"Come right up, Paul. And so this is your mother. I am very glad to see you, Mrs. Hoffman. Come right up, and I'll do all I can to make you comfortable."

"I am afraid we shall give you trouble, Mrs. Norton," said Mrs. Hoffman.

"Not in the least. The more the merrier, that's my motto. I haven't got much to offer, but what there is you are very welcome to."

The room into which they were ushered was covered with a plain, coarse carpet. The chairs were wooden, but there was a comfortable rocking-chair, a cheap lounge, and a bookcase with a few books, besides several prints upon the wall. Sam's father was a policeman, while his mother was a New England woman of good common-school education, neat and thrifty, and so, though their means were small, she managed to make a comfortable home. Mrs. Hoffman looked around her with pleased approval. It was pleasant to obtain even temporary refuge in so homelike a place.

17

"Is this your little brother who draws such fine pictures?" asked Mrs. Norton.

Jimmy looked pleased but mystified. How should Mrs. Norton have heard of his pictures?

"You must draw me a picture tonight, won't you?" asked Mrs. Norton.

"I should like to, if I can have a pencil and some paper. All mine are burned up."

"Sam will give you some from his desk. But you must be hungry."

Sam was drawn aside by his mother, and, after a whispered conference, was dispatched to the butcher's and baker's, when he soon returned with a supply of rolls and beefsteak, from which in due time an appetizing meal was spread, to which all did full justice.

CHAPTER IV

THE POLICEMAN'S HOME

It was not till later in the evening that Mr. Norton came in. He had been on duty all day, and tonight he was free. Though one of the constituted guardians of the public peace, he was by no means fierce or formidable at home, especially after he had doffed his uniform, and put on an old coat.

**A period New York Municipal Police officer.
Much like Mr. Norton.**

"Edward," said his wife, "this is Paul's mother, who was burned out today. So I have asked her to stay here till she can find a place of her own."

"That is right," said the policeman. "Mrs. Hoffman, I am glad to see you. Paul has been here before. He is one of Sam's friends."

"Paul likes to keep in with father," said Sam slyly, "considering he is on the police."

"If he is to be known by the company he keeps," said Mr. Norton, "he might have to steer clear of you."

Here I may explain why Sam was a newsboy, though his father was in receipt of a salary as a policeman. He attended school regularly, and only spent about three hours daily in selling papers, but this gave him two or three dollars a week, more than enough to buy his clothes. The balance he was allowed to deposit in his own name at a savings-bank. Thus he was accumulating a small fund of money, which by and by might be of essential use to him.

The group that gathered around the dinner table was a lively one, although half the party had been burned out. But Paul knew he was in a position to provide a new home for his mother, and thus was saved anxiety for the future.

"You have very pleasant rooms, Mrs. Norton," said Mrs. Hoffman.

"Yes, we have as good as we can afford. Twenty dollars a month is a good deal for us to pay, but then we are comfortable, and that makes us work more cheerfully."

"How do you like being a policeman, Mr. Norton?" asked Paul.

"I don't like it much, but it pays as well as anything I can get."

"I sometimes feel anxious about him," said Mrs. Norton. "He is liable to be attacked by ruffians at any time. The day he came home with his face covered with blood, I was frightened then, I can tell you."

"How did it happen?"

"I was called in to arrest a man who was beating his wife," said the policeman. "He was raging with drink at the time. He seized one of his wife's flatirons and threw it at me. It was a stunner. However, I managed to arrest him, and had the satisfaction of knowing that he would be kept in confinement for a few months. I have to deal with some tough customers. A policeman down in this part of the city has to take his life in his hand. He never knows when he's going to have a stormy time."

"I wish my husband were in some other business," said Mrs. Norton.

"There are plenty of men that would like my position," said her husband. "It's sure pay, and just as good in dull times as in good. Besides, some people think it's easy work, just walking around all day. They'd better try it."

"There's one part Mr. Norton likes," said his wife slyly. "It's showing ladies across the street."

"I don't know about that," rejoined the policeman. "It gets rather monotonous crossing the street continually, and there's some danger in it too. Poor Morgan was run over only three months ago, and injured so much that he's been obliged to leave the force. Then some of the ladies get frightened when they're halfway over, and make a scene. I remember one old woman, who let go my arm, and ran screaming in among the carriages, and it was a miracle that she didn't get run over. If she had clung to me, she'd have got over all right."

"I don't think I'll be a policeman," said Sam. "I might have to take you up, Paul, and I shouldn't like to do that."

"Paul isn't bad," said Jimmy, who was very apt to take a joke seriously, and who always resented any imputation upon his brother. "He never got took up in his life."

"Then he wasn't found out, I suppose," said Sam.

"He never did anything bad," retorted Jimmy indignantly.

"Thank you, Jimmy," said Paul, laughing. "I'll come to you when I want a first-class recommendation. If I never did anything bad, I suppose you won't call that horse bad that I drew the other day."

"It was a bad picture," said the little boy; "but people don't get took up for making bad pictures."

"That's lucky," said Sam, "or I shouldn't stand much chance of keeping out of the station-house. I move Jimmy gives us a specimen of his skill. I've got a comic paper here somewhere. He can copy a picture out of that."

"Where is it?" asked Jimmy eagerly.

The paper was found, and the little boy set to work with great enthusiasm, and soon produced a copy of one of the pictures, which was voted excellent. By that time he was ready to go to bed. Paul and he had to take up with a bed on the floor, but this troubled them little. They felt thankful, under the circumstances, to have so comfortable a shelter. Indeed, Jimmy troubled himself very little about the future. He had unbounded faith in Paul, to whom he looked up with as much confidence as he would have done to a father.

Early the next morning Mr. Norton was obliged to enter upon his daily duties. The poor must be stirring betimes, so they all took an early breakfast.

"Mother," said Paul, "it won't be much use to look up new rooms before the middle of the forenoon. I think I will open my stand as usual, and return at ten, and then we can go out together."

"Very well, Paul. I will help Mrs. Norton, if she will let me, till then."

"There is no need of that, Mrs. Hoffman."

"I would rather do it. I want to make some return for your kindness."

So the two women cleared away the breakfast dishes and washed them, and then Mrs. Hoffman sewed for two hours upon a shirt which his mother had commenced for Sam. Jimmy amused himself by copying another picture from the comic paper before mentioned.

Meantime Paul got out his stock in trade, and began to be on the watch for customers. He bought a copy of the Herald from his friend Sam, and began to pore over the advertisements headed "FURNISHED ROOMS AND APARTMENTS TO LET."

"Let me see," soliloquized Paul; "here are four elegantly furnished rooms on Fifth Avenue, only fifty dollars a week, without board. Cheap enough! But I'm afraid it would be rather too far away from my business."

"I suppose that's the only objection," said Sam slyly.
"There might be one or two others, Sam. Suppose you pick out something for me."

"What do you say to this, Paul?" said Sam, pointing out the following advertisement:

"FURNISHED NEATLY FOR HOUSEKEEPING. Front parlor, including piano, with front and back bedrooms on second floor; front basement; gas, bath, hot and cold water, stationary tubs; rent reasonable. West Twenty-seventh Street."

"That would be very convenient, especially the piano and the stationary tubs," observed Paul. "If I decide to take the rooms, you can come round any time and practice on the tubs."

"Thank you, Paul, I think I'd rather try the piano."

"I thought you might be more used to the tubs. However, that's too far uptown for me."

"Are you going to get furnished rooms?"

"I haven't spoken to mother about it, but as we have had all our furniture burned up, we shall probably get furnished rooms at first."

"Perhaps this might suit you, then," said Sam, reading from the paper:

"TO LET—FOR HOUSEKEEPING, several nicely furnished rooms; terms moderate. Apply at — Bleecker Street."

"That must be near where Barry used to live."

"Would it be too far?"

"No, I don't think it would. It isn't far to walk from Bleecker Street. But it will depend a little on the terms."

"Terms moderate," read off Sam.

"They might call them so, even if they were high."

"I wish there were some rooms to let in our building."

"I shouldn't mind taking them if they were as nice as yours. How long have you lived there?"

"We only moved on the first day of May."

"How much do you charge for your neckties, boy?" asked a female voice.

Looking up, Paul beheld a tall, hard-visaged female, who had stopped in front of his stand.

"Twenty-five cents," answered Paul.

"Seems to me they're rather high," returned the would-be customer. "Can't you sell me one for twenty cents?"

"I never take less than twenty-five, madam."

"I am looking for a nice birthday present for my nephew," said the hard-visaged lady, "but I don't want to spend too much. If you'll say twenty cents, I'll take two."

"I'm sorry, but I have only one price," said the young merchant.

"I'll give you twenty-two cents."

"I shall have to charge twenty-five."

"I suppose I must pay it then," said the lady in a dissatisfied tone. "Here, give me that blue one."

The necktie was wrapped up, and the money reluctantly paid.

"How would you like to be her nephew, Sam?" asked Paul, as soon as she was out of hearing. "You might get a nice birthday present now and then."

"Shouldn't wonder if that twenty-five cents bust the old woman! Do you often have customers like that?"

"Not very often. The other day a young man, after wearing a necktie for a week, came back, and wanted to exchange it for one of a different color."

"Did you exchange it?"

"I guess not. I told him that wasn't my style of doing business. He got mad, and said he'd never buy anything more of me."

"That reminds me of a man that bought a Tribune from me early in the morning, and came back after reading it through and wanted to exchange it for a Times. But I must be goin', or I'll be stuck on some of my papers."

CHAPTER V

HOUSE HUNTING

At ten o'clock Paul closed up his business for the forenoon, and returning to their temporary home, found his mother waiting for him.

"Well, Paul," she said inquiringly, "have you heard of any good rooms?"

"Here is an advertisement of some nicely furnished rooms on Bleecker Street;" and Paul pointed to the Herald.

"They may be above our means, Paul."

"At any rate we can go and look at them. We must expect to pay more if we take them furnished."

"Do you think we had better take furnished rooms?" asked Mrs. Hoffman doubtfully.

"I think so, mother, just now. All our furniture is burned, you know, and it would take too much of our capital to buy new. When we get richer we will buy some nice furniture."

"Perhaps you are right, Paul. At any rate we will go and look at these rooms."

"If they don't suit us, I have the paper with me, and we can look somewhere else."

"May I go, mother?" asked Jimmy.

"We might have to go about considerably, Jimmy," said Paul. "I am afraid you would get tired."

"If Mrs. Norton will let you stay here, I think it will be better," said his mother. "Are you sure he won't be in your way, Mrs. Norton?"

"Bless his heart, no," returned the policeman's wife heartily. "I shall be glad of his company. Mr. Norton and Sam are away most of the time, and I get lonely sometimes."

Jimmy felt rather flattered by the thought that his company was desired by Mrs. Norton, and readily resigned himself to stay at home. Paul and his mother went out, and got on board a Bleecker street car, which soon brought them to the desired number.

The house was quite respectable in appearance, far more so certainly than the burned tenement house. The time had been when Bleecker Street was fashionable, and lined with the dwellings of substantial and prosperous citizens. That time had gone by. Still it was several grades above the streets in the lower part of the city.

Paul rang the bell, and the door was opened by a maid-servant.

"I saw an advertisement in the Herald about some rooms to let," said Paul. "Can we see them?"

"I'll speak to the mistress," was the reply. "Won't you come in?"

They entered the hall, and were shown into the parlor, where they took seats on a hard sofa. Soon the door opened, and a tall lady entered.

"You would like to look at my rooms?" she inquired, addressing Mrs. Hoffman.

"If you please."

"They are on the third floor—all that I have vacant. If you will follow me, I will show you the way."

At the top of the second staircase she threw open the door of a good-sized room, furnished plainly but neatly.

"There is another room connected with this," she said, "and a bedroom on the upper floor can go with it."

"Is it arranged for housekeeping?" asked Mrs. Hoffman.

"Yes; you will find the back room fitted for cooking. Come in and I will show you."

She opened a door in the rear room, displaying a pantry and sink, while a cooking-stove was already put up. Both rooms were carpeted. In the front room there was a sofa, a rocking-chair, some shelves for books, while three or four pictures hung from the walls.

"I don't see any sleeping accommodations," said Mrs. Hoffman, looking around.

"I will put a bed into either room," said the landlady. "I have delayed doing it till the rooms were let."

"How do you like it, mother?" asked Paul.

"Very well, but——"

Mrs. Hoffman hesitated, thinking that the charge for such accommodations would be beyond their means. Paul understood, and asked in his turn:

"How much do you ask for these rooms by the month?"

"With the small room upstairs besides?"

"Yes."

"Thirty dollars a month."

Mrs. Hoffman looked at Paul in dismay. This was five times what they had been accustomed to pay.

"We can afford to pay more than we have hitherto," he said in a low voice. "Besides, there is the furniture."

"But thirty dollars a month is more than we can afford," said his mother uneasily.

"My mother thinks we cannot afford to pay thirty dollars," said Paul.

"The price is very reasonable," said the landlady. "You won't find cheaper rooms on this street."

"I don't complain of your price," said Mrs. Hoffman, "only it is more than we can afford to pay. Could you take less?"

"No," said the landlady decidedly. "I am sure to get tenants at that price."

"Then, Paul, I think we must look further," said his mother.

"If you don't find anything to your mind, perhaps you will come back," suggested the landlady.

"We may do so. How much would you charge for these two rooms alone?"

"Twenty-six dollars a month."

The prices named above are considerably less than the present rates; but still, as Paul's income from his business only amounted to fifty or sixty dollars a month, it seemed a good deal for him to pay.

"We may call again," said Mrs. Hoffman as they went downstairs. "But we will look around first."

"How much do you think we can afford to pay, Paul?" asked Mrs. Hoffman.

"We can easily afford twenty dollars a month, mother."

"That is more than three times as much as we pay now."

"I know it, but I want a better home and a better neighborhood, mother. When we first took the other rooms, six dollars a month was all we were able to pay. Now we can afford better accommodations."

"What other rooms have you got on your list, Paul?"

"There are some rooms on Prince Street, near Broadway."

"I am afraid they would be too high-priced."

"At any rate we can go and look at them. They are nearby."

The rooms on Prince Street proved to be two in number, well furnished, and though not intended for housekeeping, could be used for that purpose. The rent was twenty-five dollars a month.

"I do not feel able to pay more than twenty dollars," said Mrs. Hoffman.

"That is too little. I'll split the difference and say twenty-two and a half. I suppose you have no other children?"

"I have one other—a boy of eight."

"Then I don't think I should be willing to let you the rooms," said the landlady, her manner changing. "I don't like to take young children."

"He is a very quiet boy."

"No boys of eight are quiet," said the landlady decidedly. "They are all noisy and troublesome."

"Jimmy is never noisy or troublesome," said Mrs. Hoffman, resenting the imputation upon her youngest boy.

"Of course you think so, as you are his mother," rejoined the landlady. "You may be mistaken, you know."

"Perhaps you object to me also," said Paul. "I am more noisy than my little brother."

"I look upon you as a young man," said the landlady—a remark at which Paul felt secretly complimented.

"I think we shall have to try somewhere else, mother," he said. "Perhaps we shall find some house where they don't object to noisy boys."

It seemed rather a joke to Paul to hear Jimmy objected to as noisy and troublesome, and for some time afterward he made it a subject for joking Jimmy. The latter took it very good-naturedly and seemed quite as much amused as Paul.

The Herald had to be consulted once more. Two other places nearby were visited, but neither proved satisfactory. In one place the rooms were not pleasant, in the other case the price demanded was too great.

"It's twelve o'clock already," said Paul, listening to the strokes of a neighboring clock. "I had no idea it was so hard finding rooms. I wonder whether Mrs. Norton would keep us a day longer."

"Perhaps we can go out this afternoon and prove more successful, Paul."

"I've a great mind to consult Mr. Preston, mother. I think I'll call at his place of business at any rate, as I may need to draw some of the money we have in his hands. You know we've all got to buy new clothes."

"Very well, Paul. Do as you think best. You won't need me."

"No, mother."

Mrs. Hoffman returned to her temporary quarters, and reporting her want of success, was cordially invited by Mrs. Norton to remain as her guest until she succeeded in obtaining satisfactory rooms.

CHAPTER VI

PAUL TAKES A HOUSE ON

MADISON AVENUE

Paul kept on his way to the office of Mr. Preston. Those who have read the previous volume will remember him as a gentleman whose acquaintance Paul had made accidentally. Attracted by our hero's frank, straightforward manner and manly bearing, he had given him some work for his mother, and on other occasions had manifested an interest in his welfare. He now held one hundred and fifty dollars belonging to Paul, or rather to Mrs. Hoffman, for which he allowed legal interest.

On entering the mercantile establishment, of which Mr. Preston was at the head, Paul inquired for him of one of the salesmen.

"He is in his office," said the latter.

"Can I see him?"

"I don't know. Do you want to see him personally?"

"Yes, if he has time to see me."

"From whom do you come?"

"I come on my own business."

"Then I don't think you can see him," said the clerk, judging that a boy's business couldn't be very important.

"If you will be kind enough to carry in my name," said Paul, "Mr. Preston will decide that."

Paul happened to have in his pocket a business card of the firm from which he bought the silk used in making up his neckties. He wrote on the back his name, PAUL HOFFMAN, and presented it to the clerk.

The latter smiled a little superciliously, evidently thinking it rather a joke that a boy of Paul's age should think himself entitled to an interview with Mr. Preston during business hours, and on business of his own. However, he took the card and approached the office.

"There's a boy outside wishes to see you, Mr. Preston," he said.

"From whom does he come?" asked his employer, a portly, pleasant-looking gentleman.

"On business of his own, he says. Here is his card."

"Oh, to be sure. Paul Hoffman!" repeated Mr. Preston, glancing at the card. "Tell him to come in."

"I wonder what business he can have with Mr. Preston," thought the clerk, considerably surprised.

"You can go in," he said on his return.

Paul smiled slightly, for he observed and enjoyed the other's surprise.

"Well, my young friend," said Mr. Preston cordially, "how are you getting on?"

"Pretty well in business, sir," answered Paul. "But we got burned out yesterday."

"How burned out?"

"I mean the tenement house in which we lodged was burned down."

"No one injured, I hope."

"No, sir; but we lost what little we had there."

"Were you at home at the time?"

"No, sir; my mother and little brother and myself were at Barnum's Museum. But for that we might have saved some of our clothing."

"Well, have you got a new place?" "No, sir; we are stopping at the rooms of some friends. I am looking out for some furnished rooms, as I don't want to buy any new furniture. As all our clothes are burned, I may have to draw fifty dollars of the money in your hands."

"How much rent do you expect to pay?"

"I suppose we must pay as much as twenty dollars a month for comfortable furnished rooms."

"Can you afford that?"

"My business brings me in as much as fifty dollars a month."

"You haven't engaged rooms yet?"

"No, sir; my mother and I went out to look at some this morning. We only saw one place that suited us. That we could have got for twenty-two dollars and a half rent, but when they heard of my little brother they wouldn't take us."

"I see. Some persons object to young children. I am glad you have not engaged a place yet."

Paul looked at Mr. Preston inquiringly.

30

"A gentleman of my acquaintance," proceeded the merchant, "is about sailing to Europe with his family. He is unwilling to let his house, fearing that his furniture would be injured. Besides, the length of his stay is uncertain, and he would want to go into it at once if he should return suddenly. What I am coming to is this. He wants some small family to go in and take care of the house while he is away. They would be allowed to live in the basement and use the chambers on the upper floor. In return they would receive the rent free. How would your mother like to make such an arrangement?"

"Very much," answered Paul promptly. He saw at a glance that it would be a great thing to save their rent, amounting, at the sum they expected to pay, to more than two hundred and fifty dollars a year. "Where is the house?"

"It is on Madison Avenue, between Thirty-third and Thirty-fourth streets.

This was a considerable distance uptown, about three miles away from his place of business; but then Paul reflected that even if he rode up and down daily in the cars the expense would be trifling, compared with what they would save in house-rent. Besides, it would be rather agreeable to live on so fashionable a street.

"Do you think my mother can get the chance?" he asked.

"I think so. The gentleman of whom I spoke, Mr. Talbot, expects to sail for Europe next Wednesday, by the Cunard Line. So the matter must be decided soon."

"Shall I call upon Mr. Talbot," asked Paul, "or shall you see him?"

"Here he is, by good luck," said Mr. Preston, as the door opened and an elderly gentleman entered. "Talbot, you are just the man I want to see."

"Indeed! I am glad to hear that. What is it?"

"Have you arranged about your house yet?"

"No; I came in partly to ask if you knew of any trustworthy family to put in while I am away."

"I can recommend someone who will suit you, I think," returned Mr. Preston. "The young man at your side."

"He hasn't got a family already?" inquired Mr. Talbot, with a humorous glance at our hero. "It seems to me he is rather forward."

"I believe not," said Mr. Preston, smiling; "but he has a mother, a very worthy woman, and a little brother. As for my young friend himself, I can recommend him from my own knowledge of his character. In fact, he has done me the honor of making me his banker to the extent of a hundred and fifty dollars."

"So that you will go bail for him. Well, that seems satisfactory. What is his name?"

"Paul Hoffman."

"Are you in a counting-room?" asked Mr. Talbot, turning to Paul

"No, sir; I keep a necktie stand below the Astor House."

"I must have seen you in passing. I thought your face looked familiar. How much can you make now at that?"

"From twelve to fifteen dollars a week, sir."

"Very good. That is a good deal more than I made at your age."

"Or I," added Mr. Preston. "Paul was burned out yesterday," he added, "and is obliged to seek a new home. When he mentioned this to me, I thought at once that you could make an arrangement for your mutual advantage." "I shall be glad to do so," said Mr. Talbot. "Your recommendation is sufficient, Mr. Preston. Do you understand the terms proposed?" he continued, addressing Paul.

"Yes, sir, I think so. We are to have our rent free, and in return are to look after the house."

"That is right. I don't wish the house to remain vacant, as it contains furniture and articles of value, and an empty house always presents temptations to rogues. You will be free to use the basement and the upper floor. When the rest of the house needs cleaning, or anything of that kind, as for instance when I am about to return, it will be done under your or your mother's oversight, but I will pay the bills. Directions will be sent you through my friend Mr. Preston."

"All right, sir," said Paul. "How soon would you wish us to come?"

"I would like you and your mother to call up this evening and see Mrs. Talbot. You can move in next Tuesday, as we sail for Europe on the following day."

"Yes, sir," said Paul in a tone of satisfaction.

"I will expect you and your mother this evening. My number is
——."

"We will be sure to call, sir."

Mr. Talbot now spoke to Mr. Preston on another topic.

"Oh, by the way, Paul," said Mr. Preston in an interval of the conversation, "you said you wanted fifty dollars."

"I don't think I shall need it now, Mr. Preston," answered Paul. "I have some other money, but I supposed I might have to pay a month's rent in advance. Now that will not be necessary. I will bid you good-morning, sir."

"Good-morning, Paul. Call on me whenever you need advice or assistance."

"Thank you, sir; I will."

"That's what I call a good day's work," said Paul to himself in a tone of satisfaction. "Twenty dollars a month is a good deal to save. We shall grow rich soon at that rate."

He determined to go home at once and announce the good news. As he entered the room his mother looked up and inquired:

"Well, Paul, what news?"

"I've engaged a house, mother."

"A house? Where?"

"On Madison Avenue."

"You are joking, Paul."

"No, I am not, or if I am, it's a good joke, for we are really to live in a nice house on Madison Avenue and pay no rent at all."

"I can't understand it, Paul," said his mother, bewildered.

Paul explained the arrangement which he had entered into. It is needless to say that his mother rejoiced in the remarkable good luck which came to them just after the misfortune of the fire, and looked forward with no little pleasure to moving into their new quarters.

CHAPTER VII

THE HOUSE ON MADISON AVENUE

In the evening, as had been agreed, Paul accompanied his mother uptown to call on Mrs. Talbot and receive directions in regard to the house. They had no difficulty in finding it. On ringing the bell they were ushered into an elegantly furnished parlor, the appearance of which indicated the wealth of the owner.

"Suppose we give a party, mother, after we move in," said Paul, as he sat on the sofa beside his mother, awaiting the appearance of Mrs. Talbot.

"Mrs. Talbot might have an objection to our using her parlors for such a purpose."

"I wonder," said Paul reflectively, "whether I shall ever have a house of my own like this?"

"Not unless your business increases," said his mother, smiling.

"I rather think you are right, mother. Seriously, though, there are plenty of men in New York, who live in style now, who began the world with no better advantages than I. You see there is a chance for me too."

"I shall be satisfied with less," said his mother. "Wealth alone will not yield happiness."

"Still it is very comfortable to have it."

"No doubt, if it is properly acquired."

"If I am ever rich, mother, you may be sure that I shall not be ashamed of the manner in which I became so."

"I hope not, Paul."

Their conversation was interrupted by the entrance of Mrs. Talbot. She was a stout, comely-looking woman of middle age and pleasant expression.

"I suppose this is Mrs. Hoffman," she said.

Paul and his mother both rose.

"I am Mrs. Hoffman," said the latter. "I suppose I speak to Mrs. Talbot?"

"You are right. Keep your seat, Mrs. Hoffman. Is this your son?"

Paul bowed with instinctive politeness, and his mother replied in the affirmative.

"Mr. Talbot tells me that you are willing to take charge of the house while we are absent in Europe."

"I shall be glad to do so."

"We have been looking out for a suitable family, and as our departure was so near at hand, were afraid we might not succeed in making a satisfactory arrangement. Fortunately Mr. Preston spoke to my husband of you, and this sets our anxiety at rest."

"I hope I may be able to answer your expectations, Mrs. Talbot," said Mrs. Hoffman modestly.

"I think you will," said Mrs. Talbot, and she spoke sincerely.

She had examined her visitor attentively, and had been very favorably impressed by her neat dress and quiet, lady-like demeanor. She had been afraid, when first informed by her husband of the engagement he had made, that Mrs. Hoffman might be a coarse, untidy woman.

"I suppose," she said, "you would like to look over the house."

"Thank you, I should."

"I also wish you to see it, that you may understand my directions in regard to the care of it. Follow me, if you please. We will first go down into the basement."

Mrs. Hoffman rose. Paul kept his seat, not sure whether he was included in the invitation or not.

"Your son can come, too, if he likes," said Mrs. Talbot, observing his hesitation.

Paul rose with alacrity and followed them. He had a natural curiosity to see the rooms they were to occupy.

They descended first into the basement, which was spacious and light. It consisted of three rooms, the one in front quite large and pleasant. It was plainly but comfortably furnished. The kitchen was in the rear, and there was a middle room between.

"These will be your apartments," said Mrs. Talbot. "Of course I have no objection to your moving in any of your own furniture, if you desire it."

"We have only ourselves to move in," said Paul. "We were burned out early this week."

"Indeed! You were unfortunate."

"I thought so at the time," said Mrs. Hoffman, "but if it had not been for that Paul would not have called upon Mr. Preston and we should not have heard of you."

"Were you able to save nothing?" asked Mrs. Talbot.

"Scarcely anything."

"If you are embarrassed for want of money," suggested Mrs. Talbot kindly, "I will advance you fifty dollars, or more if you require it."

"You are very kind," said Mrs. Hoffman gratefully; "but we have a sum of money, more than enough for our present needs, deposited with Mr. Preston. We are not less obliged to you for so kind an offer."

Mrs. Talbot was still more prepossessed in favor of her visitors by the manner in which her offer had been declined. She saw that they had too much self-respect to accept assistance unless actually needed.

"I am glad to hear that," she said. "It is not all who are fortunate enough to have a reserve fund to fall back upon. Now, if you have sufficiently examined the basement, we will go upstairs."

While passing through the upper chambers, Mrs. Talbot gave directions for their care, which would not be interesting to the reader, and are therefore omitted.

"I had intended," she said, "to offer you the use of the upper chambers, but they are so far off from the basement that it might be inconvenient for you to occupy them. If you prefer, you may move down two bedsteads to the lower part of the house. I have no objection to your putting one in the dining-room, if you desire it."

"Thank you, Mrs. Talbot; I should prefer it."

"Then you may consider yourself at liberty to do it. I believe I have now said all I wanted to you. Can you come here next Tuesday?"

"Yes, we will do so."

"By the way, I forgot to inquire the size of your family."

"I have only one other child, a little boy of eight."

Mrs. Talbot heard this with satisfaction, for she was aware of the destructive propensities of children, and preferred that the family in charge should be small.

"I believe I have nothing further to say," said Mrs. Talbot. "Should anything else occur to me, I will mention it to you on Tuesday when you come here permanently."

Paul and his mother took their leave. When they were in the street, Paul inquired:

"Well, mother, what do you think of Mrs. Talbot?"

"I like her very much. She seems to be a real lady."

"So I think. She seems to be very kind and considerate."

"We are very fortunate to get so good a home and save the entire rent."

"It will save us two hundred and forty dollars a year."

"We shall be able to save up considerable money every year."

"But there's one thing I want to say, mother. As we are in so much better circumstances, there will be no need of your working on neckties any more."

"Are you going to discharge me from your employment, Paul?" said his mother, smiling.

"Not unless you are willing, mother; but you will have enough to do looking after the house."

"I would rather keep on making neckties. It is a work that I like. In return I will hire my washing done, and all the rougher work."

"Perhaps that will be better," said Paul; "but you can do both if you like."

"I don't mean to lead an idle life, Paul. I should not feel happy if I did. I was always fond of sewing—that is, in moderation. When I made shirts for that establishment on Broadway, for such low prices, I cannot say that I enjoyed that very much. I am glad to be relieved of such work, though at that time I was glad to get it."

"Those days have gone by forever, I hope, mother. I am young and strong, and I don't see why there isn't as good a chance for me to succeed as for other poor boys who have risen to wealth and eminence. I am going to work for success, at any rate. But we shall have to make some purchases before Tuesday."

"What kind of purchases?"

"Jimmy and I are out of clothes, you know. My entire wardrobe has been consumed by the devouring element, as the reporters say. Now, being a young man of fashion, I don't quite like being reduced to one suit and one shirt, with other things in proportion."

"If you could wait, I would make you some shirts."

"But I can't wait. I shouldn't feel like wearing the shirt I have on more than a fortnight."

"I hope not," said his mother, smiling.

"Suppose I should be invited to a party and be obliged to decline with thanks, on account of having only one shirt. My reputation as a young man of fashion would be gone forever."

"So I should think."

"Tomorrow I will buy a couple of shirts, and these will last me, with the help of the washerwoman, until you can make me some new ones. Then I will go to Bookair's tomorrow, and take Jimmy with me and buy new suits for both."

"I am afraid you are getting extravagant, Paul."

"If we live on Madison Avenue, we must dress accordingly, you know, mother. That reminds me, I must buy two trunks also."

"Two?"

"Yes; one for you, and the other for Jimmy and myself. At present I could tie up all my clothes in a handkerchief—that is, if I had a spare one; but I am going to have some more. You must have some new things also, mother."

"I can wait till we get settled in our new home. I am afraid you won't have money enough for all the articles you mean to buy."

"I may have to draw some from Mr. Preston. I think I will call on him tomorrow and do so. I forgot how much we had to buy. I shall close up business tomorrow and Monday, and spend the time in preparation for moving."

Mrs. Hoffman would not, had the matter rested with her, have been in favor of expending so much money, but she had considerable confidence in Paul's judgment, and indeed their prospects looked bright enough to warrant it; so she withdrew her objections, and Paul had his own way, as he generally did.

CHAPTER VIII

A GIFT

The next forenoon Paul called at Mr. Preston's place of business. On entering the office he found Mr. Talbot conversing with him.

"Talbot," said Mr. Preston, "this is your new tenant, Paul Hoffman."

"Good-morning, Paul," said Mr. Talbot pleasantly. "Mrs. Talbot tells me that you and your mother called last evening."

"Yes, sir."

"I was called away by an engagement, but I am glad to say that Mrs. Talbot approves my choice."

"Thank you, sir."

"I hear from Mr. Preston that you have been unfortunate in being burned out."

"Yes, sir, we have been burned out, but we hadn't much to lose."

"Were you able to save any of your clothing?"

"My mother saved a new dress she had just bought."

"Was that all?"

"Yes, sir."

"It will cost you considerable to replace what was destroyed."

"Considerable for me, sir. I called this morning to ask Mr. Preston for fifty dollars, from the money he has of mine, to spend for clothes for my mother, and brother, and myself."

"Will fifty dollars be sufficient?"

"I have some money on hand. That will be all I shall need to draw."

"It will be a pity to disturb your savings. Your care of my house will be worth more than the rent. I will give you fifty dollars besides."

Suiting the action to the word, Mr. Talbot took out his wallet and drew therefrom five ten-dollar bills, which he placed in Paul's hands.

"You are very kind," said Paul, in grateful surprise. "We felt well paid by having our rent free."

"You are quite welcome, but I ought to tell you that it is to Mrs. Talbot you are indebted rather than to myself. She suggested my giving you the money, having been much pleased with your mother's

---

appearance."

"I am very much obliged to her also, then," said Paul, "and so will be my mother when I tell her. We will try to give you satisfaction."

"I feel sure you will," said Mr. Talbot kindly.

"That is a fine boy," he said, after Paul had bidden them good-morning and left the office.

"He is an excellent boy," said Mr. Preston warmly. "He is straightforward, manly, and honest."

"How did you fall in with him?"

"He fell in with me," said Mr. Preston, laughing.

"How is that?"

"As I was turning the corner of a street downtown one day he ran into me and nearly knocked the breath out of me."

"Which prepossessed you in his favor?" inquired Mr. Talbot, smiling.

"Not at first. However, it led to a little conversation, by which I learned that he was a street candy merchant, and that some young thief had run off with all his stock in trade. He was then in hot pursuit. Learning that his mother was a seamstress and a worthy woman, I employed her to make me some shirts. I have followed the fortunes of the family, and have been Paul's adviser since then, and latterly his banker. He is now proprietor of a street-stand, and making, for a boy of his age, quite a fair income."

"Your account interests me. If I am as well satisfied as I hope to be with the family I will hereafter seek out some way of serving him."

"I am certain you will be satisfied."

The two gentlemen now conversed of other things, with which the reader has no concern.

Paul went home in high spirits, and delighted his mother and Jimmy with the gift he had received.

"Now, mother," he said, "get on your bonnet and shawl, and we'll go out shopping."

"Won't you take me too, Paul?" asked Jimmy.

"To be sure I will. I am going to buy you a suit of clothes, Jimmy."

The little boy clapped his hands. New clothes were a rarity to him, and the purchase of a new suit, therefore, would be a memorable event.

I do not propose to detail Paul's purchases. They consisted of new suits for Jimmy and himself, and a complete outfit of under garments, closing with the purchase of two plain, substantial trunks. Mrs. Hoffman deferred her own shopping till Monday.

When, later in the day, the various articles arrived, Paul regarded them with much complacency.

"It looks as if we were getting up in the world," he said.

"You deserve to succeed, Paul," said his mother. "You have been industrious and faithful, and God has prospered you."

"I have had a good mother to encourage me," said Paul, "or I should not have done so well."

"You are right to say that, Paul," said Mrs. Norton. "It isn't every boy that has a good mother."

"That is true. There are some boys I know who would do well if their mothers were not shiftless and intemperate. You remember Tommy O'Connor, mother, don't you?"

"Yes, Paul."

"I met him on Nassau Street yesterday. He was lounging about in rags, doing nothing. He asked me to lend him five cents. I asked him why he was not at work. He said his mother took all his money and spent it for drink. Then she got quarrelsome and beat him."

"How can any mother behave in that way?" said Mrs. Hoffman, shuddering.

"I don't know, but there is more than one mother that does it, though it's more likely to be the father."

The next day dawned bright and pleasant.

"Can I put on my new clothes, Paul?" asked Jimmy.

"Yes," said Paul. "It's Sunday, and we'll all put on our best clothes and go to church."

"I should like that," said the little boy, delighted.

Mrs. Hoffman readily agreed to the plan.

If of late the family had remained at home on Sunday, it was at first for want of good clothing, not from any want of respect for religious institutions. During Mr. Hoffman's life they had attended regularly, and Paul had belonged to a Sunday-school, Jimmy being too young. The church they had formerly attended being in Harlem, they could not of course go so far, but dropped into one not far from Union Square. They were shown seats by the sexton, and listened attentively to the services, though it must be confessed that Jimmy's attention was occasionally diverted to his new clothes, of which he was not a little proud. Mrs. Hoffman felt glad once more to find herself enjoying religious privileges, and determined henceforth to attend regularly.

As they were leaving the church, Paul suddenly found himself, to his surprise, next to Mr. and Mrs. Talbot, whom he had not before observed.

"Good-morning, Mr. Talbot," he said.

Mr. Talbot turned on being addressed and said:

"What, Paul, are you here?"

"Mr. Talbot, this is my mother," said Paul.

"Mrs. Hoffman," said Mr. Talbot, with as much courtesy as if he were addressing his social equal, "I am glad to make your acquaintance. My dear, this is Mrs. Hoffman."

Mrs. Talbot greeted both cordially, and made some inquiries about Jimmy. She observed with pleasure the neat appearance of the entire family, feeling sure that those who were so careful about their own appearance would be equally careful of her house. She also thought more favorably of them for their attendance at church, having herself a high respect for religious observances. Of course Paul and his mother thanked her in fitting terms for the gift which had enabled them to replace their losses by the fire.

After a brief conversation they parted, Mr. and Mrs. Talbot going uptown, while Paul and his mother had nearly two miles to walk in a different direction.

"Next Sunday we shall be walking uptown also," said Paul. "It will look well in the Directory, 'Paul Hoffman, merchant; house, Madison Avenue,' won't it?"

"Yes," said his mother, "so long as it doesn't mention that you live in the basement."

"Some time I hope to occupy a whole house of my own."

"On Madison Avenue?"

"Perhaps so; who knows?"

"I see, Paul, you are getting ambitious."

"Where shall I be, Paul?" asked Jimmy, who felt that his future prospects deserved consideration.

"Oh, you'll be a famous artist, and have a studio on Fifth Avenue."

"Do you think so, Paul?" asked the little fellow seriously.

"I hope so. All you want is a little help from me now and then. If I had time I would give you a course of lessons in drawing."

"You draw awfully, Paul."

"Do you draw any better?"

"Of course I do."

"Mother," said Paul, with much gravity, "that boy's self-conceit is unbounded. You ought to talk to him about it."

But though Paul liked to joke Jimmy, he had already decided, after they moved uptown, to give him an opportunity of developing his talent by engaging a drawing teacher for him. The large saving in their expenses from not being obliged to pay rent would allow him to do this easily. He had not yet mentioned this to Jimmy, for he meant to surprise him.

CHAPTER IX

JULIUS

At the time appointed, Paul and his mother moved into their new home. It was necessary to buy but a small quantity of new furniture, as Mrs. Talbot authorized them to take down from the upper rooms anything of which they had need. She was led to this offer by the favorable opinion she had formed of Mrs. Hoffman. With the exception, therefore, of some bedding and a rocking-chair, the latter purchased nothing.

It took a little time, of course, to get accustomed to their new quarters. When, however, they had got to feel at home, they enjoyed them. It was no longer possible, of course, for Paul to come home to the noonday meal, since the distance between his place of business and the house on Madison Avenue was two miles and a half. He therefore was accustomed to take his lunch at a restaurant, for his mother had adopted the common New York custom of having lunch at the end of the day.

It was about six weeks after Paul's removal to Madison Avenue that one day, on approaching the restaurant on Fulton Street where he proposed to lunch, his attention was drawn to a famished-looking boy who was looking in at the window at the viands within. It was impossible to misinterpret his hungry look. Paul understood it at once, and his heart was stirred with compassion. His own prosperity had not hardened him, but rendered him more disposed to lend a helping hand to those more needy.

"Are you hungry, Johnny?" he asked.

The boy turned at the sound of the words.

"Ain't I just?" he said.

"Didn't you have any breakfast?"

"I had a piece of bread."

"Was that all?"

"Yes,"

"Could you eat a plate of meat if I gave you some?"

"Try me and see," was the reply.

"Come in, then," said Paul.

"Will you pay for it?" asked the young Arab, almost incredulous.

"Yes, I will pay for it."

44

The boy waited for no further assurance. He was not in a position to refuse so advantageous a proposal. He shuffled in, therefore, directly behind Paul.

It was not an aristocratic eating-house, but its guests were well-dressed, and the ragged boy at once attracted unfavorable attention.

"Get out of here!" said a waiter.

"He told me to come in," said the boy, beginning to tremble at the thought of losing the proffered lunch.

Paul, at whom he pointed, was known at the restaurant.

"Did this boy come in with you?" asked the waiter.

"Yes," said Paul; "he's going to dine with me."

"All right."

The waiter was rather surprised at Paul's selection of a table companion, but payment being thus guaranteed, could interpose no further objections.

"Sit down there, Johnny," said Paul, indicating a seat at one of the side tables and taking the seat opposite himself.

"Now what'll you have?" he asked, handing his young guest the bill of fare.

The young Arab took it, and holding it upside down, looked at it in perplexity.

"I can't read," said he, handing it back.

"I suppose you can eat, though," said Paul. "What'll you have?"

"Anything that's good; I ain't pertikler," said the boy.

"Do you like stewed oysters?"

The boy eagerly replied in the affirmative.

"Stewed oysters for two," ordered Paul. "That'll do to begin on, Johnny. What's your real name?"

"Julius."

"Anything else?"

"That's all the name I know."

"You can take another when you need it. Did you ever hear of Julius Caesar?"

"Yes," said the boy.

Paul was a little surprised to discover the boy's range of historical information.

"What do you know about him?" he asked.

"I don't know him; I've seed him," said the boy.

**On the left is a bowl of stewed oysters.
This is what Paul buys Julius for lunch.**

"Where have you seen him?" asked Paul, rather astonished.

"Down on Baxter Street."

"Does he live there?" asked Paul.

"Yes; he keeps a barber shop there."

Evidently the young Arab supposed that Julius Caesar the barber, within the precincts of the Five Points, was the one referred to by his questioner. Paul did not explain to him his mistake.

"Have you got any father or mother?"

"No," said the boy.

"Where do you live?"

"On Centre Street."

"What do you do for a living?"

"Sometimes I black boots; sometimes I beg."

"Who do you live with?"

"Jack Morgan."

"Is he any relation to you?"

"I dunno," answered the boy.

The conversation was here interrupted. The stews were placed on the table, with a plate of crackers.

The boy's eyes glistened. He seized the spoon, and attacked his share with evident appetite.

"Poor little chap!" thought Paul, sympathetically; "he doesn't often get a good lunch. Today he shall have all he can eat."

When the boy had finished, he said: "Will you have some pudding, or would you like some more oysters?"

"I'd like the oysters, if it's all the same to you," answered Julius.

"Another stew and some apple dumpling," ordered Paul.

Julius was in appearance about twelve years of age. In reality he was fourteen, being small of his age. He had black hair and a dark complexion; his face was thin and his figure slender. He had the expression of one who was used to privation and knew how to bear it without much hope of anything better. His clothes were soiled and ragged, but his face was clean. Water was cheap, and he was unfashionably neat for the quarter in which he lived.

The stew was brought, and an extra plate of bread and butter.

"Now go ahead," said Paul. "Eat all you want."

Julius needed no other invitation. He proceeded vigorously to accomplish the work before him, and soon both bread and oysters were disposed of.

"Have you got enough?" asked Paul, smiling.

"Yes," said Julius; "I'm full."

Have you ever seen the satisfied look of an alderman as he rose from a sumptuous civic banquet? The same expression was visible on the face of the young Arab as he leaned back in his chair, with his hands thrust into his pockets.

"Then," said Paul, "we may as well be going."

The boy seized his ragged cap and followed his benefactor from the eating-house. When they reached the sidewalk, he turned to Paul and said:

"That was a bully lunch."

Paul understood that he intended to thank him, though his gratitude was not directly expressed.

"I'm glad you liked it," said he; "but I must be going now."

Julius looked after him until he turned the corner. "He's been good to me," he said to himself; "maybe I can do something for him some day.

The young Arab had had few occasions for gratitude. The world had been a hard stepmother to him. It was years since he had known father or mother, and as long as he could remember he had been under the guardianship of a social outlaw, named Jack Morgan, who preyed upon the community whenever he got a chance. Whenever he was under the ban of the law, Julius had shifted for himself, or been transferred to one of his lawless companions. The chances seemed to be in favor of Julius growing up such another as his guardian. Had he been differently constituted he would have been worse than he was. But his natural instincts were healthful, and when he had been left entirely to himself he had lived by honest industry, devoting himself to some of the street occupations which were alone open to him. His most perilous period was when Jack resumed his guardianship, as he had done a fortnight previous, on being released from a three months' residence at Blackwell's Island.

What the tie was between him and the boy was unknown. Julius knew that Jack was not his father, for the latter had never made that claim. Sometimes he vaguely intimated that Julius was the son of his sister, and consequently his nephew, but as at times he gave a different account, Julius did not know what to think. But he had always acquiesced in his guardianship, and whenever Jack was at liberty had without hesitation gone back to him.

After a brief pause Julius followed Paul to the corner, and saw him take his place beside the necktie stand. He then remembered to have seen him there before.

"I thought I know'd him," he said; "I'll remember him now."

He wandered about vaguely, having no regular occupation. He had had a blacking-box and brush, but it had been stolen, and he had not replaced it. He had asked Jack to lend him the money requisite to set him up in the business again, but the latter had put him off, intimating that he should have something else for him to do. Julius had therefore postponed seeking any other employment, beyond hovering about the piers and railway stations on the chance of obtaining a job to carry a carpetbag or valise. This was a precarious employment, and depended much more on good fortune than the business of a newsboy or bootblack. However, in the course of the afternoon Julius earned twenty-five cents for carrying a carpet-bag to French's Hotel. That satisfied him, for he was not very ambitious. He invested the greater part of it in some coffee and cakes at one of the booths in Fulton Market, and about nine o'clock, tired with his day's tramp, sought the miserable apartment on Centre Street which he shared with Jack Morgan.

A bootblack with his blackening box.
Much like the one that Julius borrowed.

CHAPTER X

A ROOM ON CENTRE STREET

In a room on the third floor of a miserable tenement house on Centre Street two men were sitting. Each had a forbidding exterior, and neither was in any danger of being mistaken for a peaceful, law-abiding citizen. One, attired in a red shirt and pants, was leaning back in his chair, smoking a clay pipe. His hair was dark and his beard nearly a week old. Over his left eye was a scar, the reminder of a wound received in one of the numerous affrays in which he had been engaged.

This was Jack Morgan, already referred to as the guardian of the boy Julius. He was certainly a disreputable-looking ruffian, and his character did not belie his looks.

The other man was taller, better dressed, and somewhat more respectable in appearance. But, like Jack, he, too, was a social outlaw, and the more dangerous that he could more easily assume an air of respectability, and pass muster, if he chose, as an honest man.

"Well, Marlowe," said Jack Morgan to the latter, who had just entered, "how's business?"

"Not very good," said Marlowe, shaking his head. "I haven't been so hard up for a long time. You haven't lost much by being shut up."

"I've had my board and lodging free," said Morgan; "but I'd rather look out for myself. I don't like free hotels." Marlowe smiled.

"That's where you're right, Jack. I never tried it but once, and then I didn't like it any better than you."

"You're a sharp one. You always cover your tracks."

"The cops don't often get hold of me," said Marlowe, with pride. "You remember that big bond robbery a year ago?"

"Yes. You wasn't in that?"

"Yes, I was."

"The rest of the fellows got trapped."

"That's so; but I heard in time and got off."

"Did you make anything out of it?"

"I made sure of a thousand-dollar bond."

"Did you put it off?"

"Yes; I sold it for half price.

"Where is the money?"

"It lasted me a month," said Marlowe, coolly. "I lived then, you can bet. But I haven't done much since. Do you see that?"

He took from his vest pocket a dollar greenback.

"What of it?"

"It's my last dollar."

"Then you've got to do something."

"Yes."

"Haven't you thought of anything?"

"I've got a plan that may work."

Here Julius entered, and his entrance produced a brief interruption. "What luck, Julius?" asked Morgan.

"Nothing much. I got a bundle to carry for a quarter."

"Have you got the money?"

"There's ten cents. I bought my supper with the rest."

"Give it to me."

Jack Morgan took the ten cents and thrust it into his pocket.

"You ain't smart, Julius," he said. "You ought to have brought more than that."

"Buy me a blacking-box and I will," said Julius.

"I'll see about it. But, Marlowe, you were just goin' to tell me of your plan."

"Shall I tell before him?" asked Marlowe, indicating the boy.

"Drive ahead. He's one of us."

"There's a house on Madison Avenue that I've heard about. It belongs to a man that's gone to Europe."

"Then there isn't much left in it worth taking."

"That's where you're wrong. I've found out that he has left all his plate locked up in a safe on the second floor and some bonds, too, it's most likely."

"Has he got much?"

"So I hear."

"Who told you?"

"A man that was in his service. He was discharged for drunkenness, and he owes this Mr. Talbot a grudge."

"Is he a thief himself?"

"No, but he is willing to help us, out of revenge."

"Then you can depend on his information."

"Yes; there is no doubt of it."

"Is the house empty?"

"No; there's a family in charge."

"That's bad."

"Not so bad; it's a widow, with two children—one a little boy of eight or thereabouts, the other sixteen."

"Do you know anything about them?"

"The oldest boy is a street peddler. He keeps a necktie stand below the Astor House."

Hitherto Julius had not taken much interest in the conversation. That his disreputable guardian should be planning a burglary did not strike him with surprise. It seemed only a matter of course. But the last remark of Marlowe put a different face upon the matter. The description was so exact that he felt almost certain the boy spoken of must be his new friend, to whom he had been indebted for the best lunch he had eaten for many a day. He began to listen now, but not too obtrusively, as that might awaken suspicion.

"A boy of sixteen may give trouble," said Jack Morgan.

"He is easily disposed of," said Marlowe, indifferently.

"I wish it were only the woman and little boy we had to deal with."

"We can easily secure the boy's absence for that night."

"How?"

"I can't tell yet, but there's plenty of ways. He might be arrested on a false charge and kept over night in the station-house. Or there's other ways. But I can't tell till I know more about him. A letter might be sent him, asking him to go over to Brooklyn."

"Wouldn't do. His mother would get somebody else in his place."

"We must find out all about him. How's that boy of yours? Is he sharp?"

"He ought to be. He's knocked about for himself long enough."

"We can try him. Come here, my son."

Julius rose from his seat and walked up to the pair.

"Hark you, my lad, can you do as you're told?"

Julius nodded.

"We've got something for you to do. It'll lead to money—do you hear?"

"I hear," said Julius.

"Have you heard what we were talking about?"

"I heard, but I didn't mind."

"Then I want you to hear, and mind, too, now. Have you ever seen a necktie stand between Dey and Cortlandt streets?"

"Yes."

"There's a boy keeps it."

"I've seed him."

"So far so good, then. Do you know anything about him?"

Julius shook his head.

"Then I want you to find out all you can about him. Find out if he's got any friends in Brooklyn, or just outside of the city. I'll tell you what I know about him, and then you must learn as much more as possible. Do you know his name?"

"No."

"It is Paul Hoffman. He and his mother live in a house that they take care of on Madison Avenue. We want to break into that house some night next week and carry off some plate and bonds that are in the safe. If we make the haul we'll do well by you."

"I understand," said Julius, nodding intelligently.

"What we want," pursued Marlowe, "is to have the boy sleep out of the house the night we make the attempt. That will leave the coast clear. If the woman wakes up and discovers us, we'll threaten to kill her if she makes any fuss. Do you hear?"

Julius nodded again.

"Do you think you can do what we want?"

"Yes."

"That's well. We'll wait for the boy's report before we lay our plans, Jack. Now that's settled, we'll send out for some whisky and drink success to the job."

"Then you must find the money, Marlowe, for I'm dead broke."

"Here, boy, take this," said Marlowe, handing Julius the bill he had recently displayed, "and bring back a pint of whisky."

"All right," said Julius.

"And mind you bring back the change, or I must go without breakfast tomorrow morning."

"I'll remember," said Julius.

When he had gone out, Marlowe said: "Where did you pick up that boy, Jack? He isn't your son, is he?"

"No; I have no son. I picked him up one day when he was a little chap. He didn't seem to belong to nobody; so I took him home, and he's been with me ever since."

"Where does he go when you are shut up, Jack? That's a good part of the time, you know."

53

"Into the streets. He picks up a living there somehow. I don't ask how."

"And he always comes back to you when you get out again?"

"Yes."

"Loves you like a father, eh?" said Marlowe, laughing.

"He's used to me," said Jack, indifferently.

Not being sentimental, he never troubled himself to expect affection from his young ward, and would not have felt very deeply afflicted if he had deserted him. Still, he, too, had got used to the society of Julius, who was the only living thing that clung to him, and probably would have felt a degree of regret at his loss. There are few, however callous, who do not feel some satisfaction in companionship.

Marlowe laughed.

"What are you laughing at?" said Jack.

"I was thinking, Jack, that you wasn't exactly the right sort to train up a boy in the way he should go, and all that. If he takes pattern by you, it's easy to tell where he'll fetch up."

"He ain't a bad sort," said Jack.

"Has he ever been over to the island?"

"No."

"Then he hasn't followed your teaching, that's all I can say."

"Never mind about the boy," said Jack, who had grown weary of the subject. "He can take care of himself."

Here Julius reappeared with the whisky. Both men brightened up at the sight of their favorite beverage.

"Have you got a pack of cards?" asked Marlowe.

"Are there any cards?" asked Jack, appealing to Julius.

The boy found some hidden away in the cupboard, and the men taking them were soon intent upon a game of poker. Julius looked on for a time, for he, too, knew something of the game; but after a time he became drowsy, and threw himself upon a pallet in the corner, which he shared with his guardian. He didn't sleep immediately, however, for now that his attention was drawn away from the game, he began to consider how he should act in the matter which had been confided to him. Should he prove true to his guardian and treacherous to Paul, or should he repay the latter for the kindness he had received at his hands? It was a difficult question. While he was pondering it his eyes closed and he fell asleep.

The men continued to play for about two hours, for penny stakes. The game had no interest for them unless something was staked upon it, and the winner pocketed his winnings with as much satisfaction as if it had been a thousand times as large.

CHAPTER XI

FREE LUNCH

About seven o'clock the next morning Julius awoke. Jack Morgan was still asleep and breathing heavily. His coarse features looked even more brutal in his state of unconsciousness. The boy raised himself on his elbow and looked thoughtfully at him as he slept.

"How did I come to be with him?" This was the question which passed through the boy's mind. "He ain't my father, for he's told me so. Is he my uncle, I wonder?"

Sometimes, but not often, this question had suggested itself to Julius; but in general he had not troubled himself much about ancestry. A good dinner was of far more importance to him than to know who his father or grandfather had been. He did not pretend to have a warm affection for the man between whom and himself existed the only tie that bound him to any fellow-creature. They had got used to each other, as Jack expressed it, and that served to keep them together when the law did not interfere to keep them apart. In general Julius had obeyed such orders as Jack gave him, but now, for the first time, a question of doubt arose in his mind. He was called upon to do something which would injure Paul, whose kindness had produced a strong impression upon him. Should he do it? This led him to consider how far he was bound to obey Jack Morgan. He could not see that he had anything to be grateful for. If Jack was flush he received some slight advantage. On the other hand, he was expected to give most of his earnings to his guardian when they were living together. While he was thinking the man opened his eyes.

"Awake, eh?" he asked.

"Yes," said Julius.

"What time is it?"

"The clock has gone seven."

"I can tell that by my stomach. I've got a healthy appetite this morning. Have you got any money?"

"Not a penny, Jack."

"That's bad. Just feel in the pocket of my breeches; there they are on the floor. See if you can find anything."

Julius rose from the pallet and did as he was ordered.

"There's twelve cents," he said.

"Good. We'll divide. We can get a breakfast at Brady's Free Lunch Saloon. Take six cents of it. I ain't going to get up yet."

"All right," said the boy.

"You must look sharp and pick up some money before night, or we shall go to bed hungry. Do you hear?"

"Yes, Jack."

"When Marlowe and I get hold of that gold and plate on Madison Avenue we'll have a grand blow-out. You remember what Marlowe told you last night?"

"About the boy that keeps the necktie stand near Dey Street?"

"Yes."

"I am to find out all I can about him."

"Yes. See if you can find out if he has any friends out of the city."

Julius nodded.

"We want to have the coast clear, so that we can break in next Monday night. The sooner the better. I'm dead broke and so is Marlowe, but I guess we can stand it till then."

"All right."

Jack Morgan turned over and composed himself to sleep again. He had said all he thought necessary, and had no pressing business to call him up. Julius opened the door and went out, down the rickety stairs and out through a narrow covered alleyway to the street, for the room which Jack Morgan and he occupied was in a rear tenement house. Several dirty and unsavory-looking children—they could not well be otherwise in such a locality—barefooted and bareheaded, were playing in the court. Julius passed them by, and sauntered along toward the City Hall Park. He met several acquaintances, newsboys and bootblacks, the former crying the news, the latter either already employed or looking for a job.

"Where are you goin', Julius?" asked a bootblack of his acquaintance.

"Goin' to get breakfast."

"Got any stamps?"

"Sixpence."

"You can't get a square meal for that."

"I'm goin' to 'free-lunch places.'"

"That's good if you're hard up. What are you doin' now?"

"Nothin' much."

"Why don't you black boots?"

"Haven't got any box or brush."

"You can borrow mine, if you'll give me half you make."

"What are you goin' to do?"

"I'll try sellin' papers for a change."

"I'll do it," said Julius, promptly, for he saw that the arrangement would, under the circumstances, be a good one for him. "Where will I see you tonight?"

"I'll be here at six o'clock."

"All right. Hand over your box." So the business arrangement was concluded—an arrangement not uncommon among street professionals. It is an illustration, on a small scale, of the advantage of capital. The lucky possessor of two or three extra blacking-boxes has it in his power to derive quite a revenue—enormous, when the amount of his investment is considered. As a general thing, such contracts, however burdensome to one party, are faithfully kept. It might be supposed that boys of ordinary shrewdness would as soon as possible save up enough to buy a box and brush of their own; but as they only receive half profits, that is not easy, after defraying expenses of lodging and meals.

Julius obtained one job before going to breakfast. He waited for another, but as none seemed forthcoming, he shouldered his box and walked down Nassau Street till he reached a basement over which was the sign, FREE LUNCH. He went downstairs and entered a dark basement room. On one side was a bar, with a variety of bottles exposed. At the lower end of the apartment was a table, containing a couple of plates of bread and butter and slices of cold meat. This was the free lunch, for which no charge was made, but it was understood to be free to those only who had previously ordered and paid for a drink. Many came in only for the drinks, so that on the whole the business was a paying one.

Julius walked up to the bar and called for a glass of lager.

"Here, Johnny," said the barkeeper.

While he was drinking, a miserable-looking man, whose outward appearance seemed to indicate that Fortune had not smiled upon him lately, sidled in, and without coming to the bar, walked up to the table where the free lunch was spread out.

"What'll you have to drink, my friend?" asked the barkeeper, pointedly.

The man looked rather abashed, and fumbled in his pockets.

"I'm out of money," he stammered.

"Then keep away from the lunch, if you please," said the proprietor of the establishment. "No lunch without a drink. That's my rule."

"I'm very hungry," faltered the man, in a weak voice. "I haven't tasted food for twenty-four hours."

"Why don't you work?"

"I can't get work."

"That's your lookout. My lunch is for those who drink first."

Julius had listened to this conversation with attention. He knew what it was to be hungry. More than once he had gone about with an empty stomach and no money to buy food. He saw that the man was weak and unnerved by hunger, and he spoke on the impulse of the moment, placing five cents in his hand.

"Take that and buy a drink."

"God bless you!" uttered the man, seizing the coin.

"What'll you have?" asked the barkeeper.

"Anything the money will buy."

A glass of lager was placed in his hands and eagerly quaffed. Then he went up to the table and ate almost ravenously, Julius bearing him company.

"God bless you, boy!" he said. "May you never know what it is to be hungry and without a penny in your pocket!"

"I've knowed it more'n once," said Julius.

"Have you—already? Poor boy! What do you do for a living?"

"Sometimes one thing—sometimes another," said Julius. "I'm blackin' boots now."

"So I am relieved by the charity of a bootblack," murmured the other, thoughtfully. "The boy has a heart."

"Can't you get nothin' to do?" asked Julius, out of curiosity.

"Yes, yes, enough to do, but no money," said the other.

"Look here," said the barkeeper, "don't you eat all there is on the table. That won't pay on a five-cent drink—that won't."

He had some cause for speaking, for the man, who was almost famished, had already eaten heartily. He desisted as he heard these words, and turned to go out.

"I feel better," he said. "I was very weak when I came in. Thank you, my boy," and he offered his hand to Julius, which the latter took readily.

"It ain't nothin'," he said, modestly.

"To me it is a great deal. I hope we shall meet again."

Street boy as he was, Julius had found some one more destitute than himself, and out of his own poverty he had relieved the pressing need of another. It made him feel lighter-hearted than usual. It was the consciousness of having done a good action, which generally brings its own reward, however trifling it may have been.

Though himself uneducated, he noticed that the man whom he had relieved used better language than was common among those with whom he was accustomed to associate, and he wondered how such a man should have become so poor.

"I don't want to see that man again," said the barkeeper. "He spends five cents and eats twenty cents' worth. If all my customers were like that, I should soon have to stop business. Do you know him?"

"Never seed him afore," said Julius.

He shouldered his box and ascended the steps to the sidewalk above. He resolved to look out for business for the next two hours, and then go around to the necktie stand of Paul Hoffman.

CHAPTER XII

A GOOD ACTION MEETS

ITS REWARD

Paul Hoffman was standing beside his stock in trade, when all at once he heard the question, so common in that neighborhood, "Shine yer boots?"

"I guess not," said Paul, who felt that his income did not yet warrant a daily outlay of ten cents for what he could easily do himself.

"I'll shine 'em for nothin'," said the boy.

Such a novel proposition induced Paul to notice more particularly the boy who made it.

"Why for nothing?" he asked, in surprise, not recognizing Julius.

"You gave me a lunch yesterday," said Julius.

"Are you the boy?" asked Paul, with interest.

"I'm the one," answered Julius. "Will you have a shine?"

"I don't want any pay for the lunch," said Paul. "You're welcome to it."

"I'd rather give you a shine," persisted Julius.

"All right," said Paul, pleased by his grateful spirit, and he put out his foot.

"Won't you let me pay for it?" asked Paul, when the job was finished and his boots were resplendent with a first-class polish.

"No," said Julius, hastily drawing back.

"Thank you, then. Have you had good luck this morning?"

"I got four shines," said Julius.

"I once blacked boots myself, for a little while," said Paul.

"You're doin' better now."

"Yes, I'm doing better now. So will you some day, I hope."

"Do you live in a house on Madison Avenue?" asked Julius, abruptly.

"Yes," said Paul, surprised. "Who told you?"

"You take care of the house for a gentleman as has gone to Europe, don't you?"

"How do you know it?" demanded Paul.

"I want to tell you something" said Julius, "only don't you never let on as I told you."

"All right. Go ahead!" said Paul, more and more mystified.

"Ain't there some gold and bonds kept in the house?"

"Why do you ask?" demanded Paul, eying the boy with suspicion.

"There's a couple of chaps that's plannin' to rob the house," said Julius, sinking his voice almost to a whisper, and looking cautiously about him to guard against being overheard.

"Who are they? How do you know it?" asked Paul, startled.

"One is Jack Morgan, the man I live with; the other is a friend of his, Tom Marlowe."

"Did you hear them talking about it?"

"Yes; last night."

"Did they tell you about it?"

"They wanted me to find out all about you—if you'd got any friends in Brooklyn, or anywheres round. They want to get you off the night they're goin' to break in."

"When is that?"

"Next Monday."

"What made you tell me all this?"

"Cause you was good to me and give me a lunch when I was hungry."

"Give me your hand," said Paul, his heart warming toward the boy who exhibited so uncommon a feeling as gratitude.

"It's dirty," said Julius, showing his hand stained with blacking.

"Never mind," said Paul, grasping it warmly. "You're a good fellow, and I'd rather take your hand than a good many that's cleaner."

Julius, rough boy as he was, looked gratified, and his face brightened. He felt that he was appreciated, and was glad he had revealed the plot.

"Now," said Paul, "you have told me about this man's plans; are you willing to help me further? Are you willing to let me know anything more that you find out about the robbery?"

"Yes, I will," said Julius, unhesitatingly.

"Then I'll depend upon you. What sort of a man is this that you live with? What's his name?"

"His name is Jack Morgan. He's a bad sort, he is. He's shut up most of the time."

"What makes you stay with him?"

"I'm used to him. There ain't nobody else I belong to."

"Is he your father?"

"No, he ain't."

"Any relation?"

"Sometimes he says he's my uncle, but maybe it ain't so—I dunno."

"Is he a strong man?"

"Yes; he's a hard customer in a fight."

"How about the other man?"

"That's Marlowe. He's the same sort. I like Jack best."

"Do you think they will try to break in next Monday night?"

"If they think you are away."

"What will you tell them?"

"What do you want me to tell them?" asked Julius, looking at him earnestly.

"I don't know," said Paul, thoughtfully. "If you should say I was going to be away, they'd want to know where, and how you found out. They might suspect something."

"That's so," said Julius.

"Suppose they heard that I would remain in the house, what would they do to prevent it?"

"They might get you took up on a false charge and put in the station-house over night, or maybe they'd seize you if they got a chance and lock you up somewhere."

"How could they have heard that Mr. Talbot left any valuables in the house?"

Julius shook his head. On that point he could give no information.

"You may tell them," said Paul, after a moment's thought, "that I have an aunt, Mrs. Green, living in Brooklyn."

"Whereabouts in Brooklyn?"

"No. 116 Third Avenue," said Paul, at a venture. "Can you remember?"

"Yes."

"They will probably send a message from her late Monday evening for me to go over there."

"Will you go?"

"I will leave the house, for they will probably be watching; but I shall not go far, and I shall leave the house well guarded."

63

Julius nodded.

"I'll tell 'em," he said.

He was about to go, when Paul called him back.

"Won't you get yourself into trouble?" he said. "I should not want to have any harm come to you."

"They won't know I'm in the game," answered Julius.

"Will you come tomorrow and let me know what they say?"

"Yes."

Julius crossed Broadway and turned onto Fulton Street, leaving Paul full of thought. He felt what a great advantage it was to be forewarned of the impending danger, since being forewarned was forearmed, as with the help of the police he could prepare for his burglarious visitors. He saw that the money he had paid for a lunch for a hungry boy was likely to prove an excellent investment, and he determined that this should not be the last favor Julius received from him.

Meanwhile Julius returned to business. With the help of his blacking materials he succeeded in earning a dollar before the close of the day. Unluckily, half of this was to be given to the young capitalist who had supplied him with a box and brush; but still fifty cents was more than he would probably have earned if he had been compelled to depend upon chance jobs. At six o'clock he met his young employer and handed over fifty cents, which the other pocketed with much satisfaction.

"Do you want to take the box ag'in tomorrow?" he asked.

"Yes," said Julius.

"All right. You can keep it then. You can take it home with you and bring me the stamps tomorrow night at this same hour."

So the contract was continued, and Julius, having treated himself to some supper, went home.

Jack Morgan was already there. He looked up as Julius entered.

"Where'd you get that box?" he asked.

"I borrowed it."

"Of a boy?"

"Yes; I give him half I makes."

"How much did you make today?"

"Ten shines. That was a dollar."

"And half of it went to you?"

"Yes, Jack."

"Where is it?"

"I had to get my lunch and dinner. There's all that's left."

He handed Jack ten cents.

"Why didn't you keep the whole of the money?" grumbled Jack. "You needn't have paid the boy."

"He'd have licked me."

"Then I'd lick him."

Julius shook his head.

"That would be cheatin'," he said. "I wouldn't want to cheat him when he give me the box."

"Oh, you're gettin' mighty particular," sneered Jack, not very well satisfied at having so large a portion of the boy's earnings diverted from himself.

"If I had a box and brush of my own I could keep all the stamps I made," said Julius.

"I'm dead broke. I can't give you no money to buy one. Did you go to see that boy I told you of?"

"Paul Hoffman?"

"Yes, if that's his name."

"Yes, I went to see him."

"And did you find out anything?" asked Jack, with eagerness.

"Yes."

"Well, out with it, then. Don't let me do all the talking."

"He's got an aunt as lives in Brooklyn."

"Whereabouts?"

"No. 116 Third Avenue."

"How did you find out?"

"I got him to talkin'."

"That's good. And did he suspect you?"

"No," said Julius.

"No. 116 Third Avenue," repeated Jack. "I must put that down. Did he tell you the name?"

"Mrs. Green."

"That's good. We'll trump up a message from her late Monday evening. I wish I knew how things was arranged in the house."

"Maybe I could go there," said Julius.

"What, to the house?"

"Yes. I could go there in the evenin' and ask him if he'd let me have some old clothes. Maybe he'd invite me upstairs, and—"

"You could use your eyes. That's a good idea, but I don't believe you'd get a chance to go up."

"Shall I try?"

"Yes; you may try tomorrow night. If we make a haul, you shall have your share. Halloo, Marlowe!"

These last words were addressed to Marlowe, who entered unceremoniously without knocking.

"I'm in luck," said Marlowe. "Here's a fiver," and he displayed a five-dollar greenback. "Come out and we'll have a jolly dinner."

Jack accepted the invitation with alacrity, communicating to his companion as they walked along the information Julius had picked up.

CHAPTER XIII

PAUL MAKES A PURCHASE

It is not very pleasant to be informed that your house is to be entered by burglars. Still, if such an event is in prospect, it is well to know it beforehand. While Paul felt himself fortunate in receiving the information which Julius gave him, he also felt anxious. However well he might be prepared to meet the attack, he did not like to have his mother and Jimmy in the house when it was made. Burglars in nearly every case are armed, and if brought to bay would doubtless use their arms, and the possible result of a chance shot was to be dreaded. On Monday night, therefore, if that should be the one decided upon by the burglars, he made up his mind that his mother and Jimmy should sleep out of the house. He lost no time in proposing this plan to his mother.

"Mother," said he on reaching home, "I have had some news today."

"Not bad, I hope?" said Mrs. Hoffman.

"I leave you to judge," answered Paul, with a smile. "We are to have visitors next Monday evening."

"Visitors, Paul? Who are they?"

"Mr. Jack Morgan and Mr. Marlowe."

"Are they friends of yours? I never heard you mention them."

"I never saw them that I know of."

"Then why did you invite them here?"

"They invited themselves."

"I don't understand it, Paul. If you don't know them, why should they invite themselves here?"

"Perhaps you'll understand me better, mother, when I tell you their business."

"What is it?"

"They are burglars."

"Burglars!" repeated Mrs. Hoffman, turning suddenly pale and sinking back into a chair, for she had been standing.

"Yes, mother. They have found out, though I can't tell how, that there are some bonds and plate in the safe upstairs, and that is their reason for coming."

"How did you find out, Paul? What a dreadful thing!" gasped Mrs. Hoffman.

"It will be worse for them than for us, I am thinking," said Paul. "It was a boy told me—a boy that lives with them. I'll tell you about it."

He gave his mother an account of what had already been communicated to him.

"Oh, dear, we shall be murdered in our beds!" exclaimed his mother, in dismal accents.

Upon this Jimmy began to cry, but Paul only laughed.

"I thought you were braver, Jimmy," he said. "If I buy you a pistol, will you promise to use it?"

"I don't know," said Jimmy, dubiously. "I should be afraid to shoot a great big man. Would he have a pistol, too?"

"Probably."

At this Jimmy began to cry again, and Paul hastened to say: "Don't be afraid; I don't mean to have you sleep in the house that night."

"Where can we go?"

"I think Mrs. Norton will let you stop with her that night.

"And you will come, too, Paul?" said Mrs. Hoffman.

"And let the house be robbed, mother? What would Mr. Talbot think of that?"

"But you will be killed. What can you do against such bad men?"

"What would you recommend, mother?" asked Paul.

"You might write a letter to them, telling them you knew all about their plan and you would have them arrested if they came."

"I don't think, mother," said Paul, laughing, "that that would be the best course. I want to get them here and catch them. Then they can be shut up, and we shall be safe from any further attempts. I am going to police headquarters, and they will tell me what to do. Probably two or three officers will be concealed in the house, and when the burglars are fairly in will arrest them."

"You needn't stay, Paul."

"It is my duty, mother. We are left by Mr. Talbot in charge of the house and what it contains. Some of us ought to be here at such a time. I will take care not to get into danger."

Mrs. Hoffman was a woman and a mother, and it was with difficulty that Paul could convince her that it was his duty to remain. At length, however, she acquiesced, and agreed to go and see Mrs. Norton the next day and ask permission to remain with her on

Monday night.

The next day Julius came to Paul's stand.

"Is there any news, Julius?" asked Paul.

"Nothin' much," said Julius. "Jack wants me to call up to your house and find out where the gold is kept."

How does he think you are going to do it without my suspecting?"

"He told me to go up and ask for some old clothes. Then, if you didn't let me into the house, I was to ask for something to eat."

"A good plan." said Paul. "When are you coming?"

"Tonight."

"Very well; I'll be ready for you. Is there any change in the evening?"

"No. They're comin' Monday night."

"I'll be ready for them," said Paul.

"What are you goin' to do?" asked Julius, and he fixed a pair of sharp, black eyes on Paul.

"Can I trust you, Julius?" demanded Paul, with a keen glance at the boy.

"Yes," said Julius.

"Then," said Paul, "I mean to have them arrested. They'll walk into a trap."

Julius looked thoughtful.

"Don't you like it, Julius?"

"I dunno," said the boy, slowly.

"Do you like this man Morgan?"

"I don't like him. I'm used to him."

"And you don't like the idea of his being arrested through your means?"

Julius nodded.

"I know how you feel, but I don't see how it can be helped. If he didn't rob us he would rob somebody else. Did he ever do any honest work?"

"Not as I knows on."

"How does he live?"

"By stealin' and gamblin'."

"I hope he won't teach you to follow his example, Julius."

"I don't want to be like him."

"Why not?"

"I want to be respectable, like you."

"You know it's wrong to steal."

"Yes," said Julius, but without any great depth of conviction. The fact is, stealing was too familiar to his observation to excite in him detestation or horror. But he was a sharp boy. He knew that his guardian for the last five years had spent more than half the time in confinement. Even when free he lived from hand to mouth. Julius had made up his mind that it did not pay. He saw that an honest mechanic got a good deal more comfort and enjoyment out of life than Jack, and he had a vague wish to become respectable. This was encouraging, as far as it went. Higher considerations might come by and by.

"If you want to be respectable, Julius, I'll help you," said Paul.

"Will you?" said Julius.

"Yes; you are doing me a great favor. I shall be in your debt, and that's the way I will pay you. You mustn't grow up like the man you live with."

"I don't want to."

"We'll talk about that after Monday. We shall have more time then."

"Shall I come up tonight, then?"

"Yes, come."

Julius strolled away with his blacking-box, and Paul was left to his reflections.

"He'll make a good boy if he's only encouraged," said Paul to himself. "I don't know what would have become of me if I'd been brought up by burglars like him. There's nothing like having a good mother. There ain't any excuse for a boy going wrong if he's got a good mother."

Paul was right. Our destinies are decided more than we know by circumstances. If the street boys, brought up to a familiarity with poverty, and often with vice and crime, go astray, we should pity as well as condemn, and if we have it in our power to make the conditions of life more favorable for any, it is our duty, as the stewards of our common Father, to do what we can.

It occurred to Paul that he had no old clothes to give Julius, all his wardrobe, not very extensive at the best, having been burned up in the fire which consumed his old home. As he had told Julius to come up, it was necessary that he should have something to give him, and he therefore decided to provide himself at a secondhand clothing store. He knew well enough where they were to be found.

His old street companions used to go to Chatham Street and Baxter Street in search of clothing, and these localities, though not distinguished for fashion, are at least reasonable in their scale of prices.

A little earlier than usual Paul closed his stand, and walked across the City Hall Park and up Chatham Street to a store he had frequently seen. Like most of its class, it had a large portion of its stock displayed outside, where the proprietor stood, keen-eyed and watchful, on the lookout for customers.

"Can I sell you something this afternoon?" he asked, obsequiously, as Paul halted in front of his store.

"That depends upon whether I see anything that suits me," answered Paul.

Before he had finished, the dealer had seized his arm, and, hurrying him into the store, pulled down a coat, on the merits of which he began to expatiate with voluble tongue.

"I don't want anything for myself," said Paul. "I want to buy a coat for a boy of twelve. Have you got anything of the right size?"

Paul need not have asked. The trader was keen at a sale, and if Barnum's giant had called for a secondhand suit, would have sworn boldly that he had the very thing. In the present case Paul found a coat which, as well as he could judge, would about fit Julius. At any rate, the street boy was not likely to be fastidious as to the quality or exact fit of a coat, which, at all events, would be a decided improvement upon the one he was now wearing.

"What is the price of this?" asked Paul.

"Five dollars," was the reply.

Paul was too well accustomed to the ways of Chatham street to pay the first price demanded, or the second or third. Finally he succeeded in getting the coat for one dollar and a half, which was cheap, although the dealer made a fair profit even at this price. Before the bargain was concluded, a tall man strayed in, and watched the bargaining with slight interest. Paul would have been not a little surprised had he known that this man was one of the burglars against whom he was contriving measures of defense. It was, indeed, Marlowe, who, having dexterously picked the pocket of a passenger on the Third Avenue cars an hour before, found himself thirty dollars richer by the operation, and being himself out at elbows, had entered this shop on an errand similar to Paul's.

"What can I sell you?" asked the shopkeeper, to his new customer.

"I want a coat," said Marlowe, roughly; "good and cheap. Don't try any of your swindling tricks on me, for I won't stand them."

With the details of the negotiation that followed we have nothing to do. It is enough to say that this chance meeting between Paul and Marlowe was not without its results, though neither knew the other.

CHAPTER XI

THE SPOT UPON THE COAT

When Julius went home at six o'clock he found Marlowe and his guardian (if Jack Morgan deserves the title) sitting over a game of cards. They looked up as he entered the room.

"Well, Julius, how are you getting on?" asked Jack. "Have you found out anything more?"

"Not yet, Jack."

"Then it's time you did."

"I'm goin' up to the house tonight."

"Does he know it?"

"Yes; he told me to come."

"What made him do that?"

"I axed him for some old clothes. He told me to come up tonight and he'd give me some."

"That's good," said Jack, approvingly. "Mind you keep your eyes open when you're there. Find out where the swag is kept. It'll save me and Marlowe some trouble."

Julius nodded.

"I'll do my best," he said.

"What time are you going up?"

"In an hour or so."

"I hope we'll make a haul, Marlowe," said Jack. "I haven't been in luck lately. If I could raise a thousand or so I'd clear out of these diggings. The cops know me too well."

"Where would you go, supposin' you got the money?" asked his companion.

"I'd go to California. They don't know me there. Something might turn up for me."

"I'll go with you, Jack, if you go. I've got tired of New York, and, as you say, they know me too well hereabouts. Will you take the boy?"

"No," said Jack carelessly. "He knows how to take care of himself. He'll be better off here."

Julius listened to this conversation, thoughtfully watching the speaker as he spoke, and it helped him to a decision in a matter that had troubled him somewhat. He could not help seeing that Jack Morgan cared nothing for him, except so far as it suited his convenience to have his companionship. Looking back, he could not see that he owed him any gratitude. The balance of favors was on the other side. He had done more for Jack than Jack for him. He asked himself if he wanted to go with Jack Morgan on this journey, and he answered his own question in the negative. It was better that he should leave him now forever. With him he could only look forward to a future of shame and disgrace.

"What are you thinking about, boy?" asked Marlowe. "Do you want to go to California with Jack and me?"

"No," answered Julius.

"Why not?"

"I'd rather stay here," answered Julius shortly.

"When I was a lad I'd have liked to go off on a journey like that."

"I like stayin' here."

"He's used to the streets," said Jack. "He likes 'em. That's best, as he can't go."

"Can you take care of yourself?" asked Marlowe.

"I always has," said Julius.

"That's so," said Jack, laughing. "You ain't given me much trouble, Julius."

The men resumed their game, and the boy looked on silently. After a while seven o'clock struck, and Julius rose from his seat.

"I'm goin'," he said.

"All right, Julius. Keep your eyes open."

"I know," said the boy.

He had saved enough money to pay for a ride uptown. He took the Fourth Avenue cars, and in half an hour found that he had reached the cross street nearest to his destination. Five minutes later he rang the basement bell of the house on Madison Avenue.

The Fourth Street Car.
Julius takes this to see Paul and his family.

Paul saw him enter the area, and went himself to open the door.

"Come in, Julius," he said. "I have been expecting you. Have you had any dinner?"

"I bought some coffee and cakes."

"I think you can eat a little more," said Paul, smiling. "Mother, can't you give Julius some dinner?"

"Is this the boy you expected, Paul?"

"Yes, mother."

"I saved some for him. Sit down at the table, Julius," she said hospitably.

Julius did as he was told, and directly Mrs. Hoffman took from the oven a plate of meat and vegetables, which had thus been kept warm, and poured out a cup of tea also. These were placed before the young Arab. His eyes lighted up with pleasure at the tempting feast, and the vigor of his assaults showed that the coffee and cakes which he had partaken had by no means destroyed his appetite. Mrs. Hoffman and Paul looked on with pleasure, glad that they had been able to give pleasure to their young visitor. Jimmy, who had heard them speak of Julius, hovered near, surveying him with curiosity. He wanted to "interview" Julius, but hardly knew how to begin. Finally he ventured to ask: "Are you the boy that lives with the robbers?"

"Jimmy!" said his mother reprovingly.

But Julius was not sensitive.

"Yes," he answered.

"Ain't you afraid of them?" continued Jimmy.

"What for?" asked Julius.

"Because robbers are bad men."

"They wouldn't hurt me," said the young Arab indifferently.

"You ain't a robber, are you?"

"No," said Julius in a matter-of-fact tone.

"What makes you live with them?"

"I haven't got anybody else to live with," said Julius.

"Are they going to rob this house?"

"Jimmy, you are talking too much," said Paul reprovingly. "I suppose they haven't changed their plans, have they, Julius?"

"No."

"They mean to come next Monday?"

"Yes."

"Did they know you were coming up here this evening?"

"Yes; I told 'em you were goin' to give me some clo'es."

"Yes," said Paul. "I've got a coat for you."

He opened a bundle and displayed the purchase he had made that afternoon on Chatham Street.

"Try it on, Julius," he said.

Julius took off the ragged coat he had on and tried on the one Paul had purchased.

"It is an excellent fit," said Mrs. Hoffman.

"Look at yourself in the glass," said Paul.

Julius surveyed himself with satisfaction. Though secondhand, the coat was decidedly superior to the one he had taken off.

"It's a bully coat," he said. "Thank you."

"You are quite welcome, Julius. You may as well wear it. You can put your old one in a paper and take it back with you."

"Jack wanted me to find out where the money was kept," said Julius.

"You may tell him it is in a safe in the front room on the second floor. But how did he expect you would find out?"

"He left that to me."

"And what will you tell him?"

"I dunno. I'll think of something."

"He won't suspect you, will he?"

"I guess not."

"Suppose he did?"

"He'd kill me," said Julius.

"What a dreadful man he must be!" exclaimed Mrs. Hoffman, shuddering. "How do you dare to live with him?"

"I shan't live with him much longer," said Julius. "He said tonight he'd go to Californy if he got swag enough here."

"What is swag?" asked Mrs. Hoffman, bewildered.

"He means money, or articles of value," explained Paul. "I don't think he'll go to California, Julius. I think he'll go somewhere else."

"I guess I'll go," said Julius, moving toward the door.

"You need not be in a hurry. We should like to have you stay longer."

"He'll expect me," said Julius.

"Go, then, if you think it best. But it is a long distance downtown, and you must be tired. Here is money to pay your fare in the cars.

"Thank yer," said Julius.

He accepted the money, and went out, first, however, promising to call upon Paul the next day at his stand and let him know whether there was any change in Jack Morgan's plans.

"I pity the poor boy," said Mrs. Hoffman, after he went out. "What a dreadful thing it is to live with such a desperate man!"

"I will see what I can do to help him next week," said Paul. "We shall owe him something for letting us know of the robbery."

"I shudder to think what might have happened if we had been taken by surprise. We might have been murdered in our beds."

Jimmy looked so frightened at this suggestion that Paul laughed.

"It is no laughing matter, mother," he said; "but Jimmy looked so thoroughly scared that I couldn't help being amused. Don't be alarmed, Jimmy. We'll take good care of you."

Meanwhile Julius was returning to the miserable room which he called home. He was thinking how he could communicate the information agreed upon without arousing the suspicions of the two confederates. Finally he decided upon a story which seemed to him satisfactory.

It was nine o'clock when he entered the room where Jack Morgan and Marlowe, having got tired of playing cards, were leaning back against the wall in their chairs, smoking clay pipes. The room was full of the odor of a villainous quality of cheap tobacco when Julius reappeared.

"Well, Julius," said Jack, removing his pipe from his mouth and regarding him eagerly, "what luck?"

"Good," said Julius briefly

"What have you found out?"

"I found out that the swag is in a safe upstairs on the second floor."

"Good!" exclaimed Jack, admiringly. "Didn't I tell you he was a sharp one, Marlowe?"

"How did you find that out?" asked Marlowe keenly. "You didn't ask, did you?"

"I ain't a fool," answered Julius.

"You haven't answered my question."

"They give me some dinner," said Julius, who had got his story ready, "and while I was eatin' I heard Mrs. Hoffman tell Paul that she had got some men to move the safe from the front room on the second floor into the bathroom. She didn't say what was in it, but it's likely the money's there."

"The boy's right, Marlowe," said Jack.

"Did they give you anything else besides dinner?" asked Marlowe.

"Yes; they give me this coat," answered Julius, indicating the coat he had on. "Ain't it a bully fit?"

"Maybe they'd like to adopt you," said Jack jocosely. "If me and Marlowe go to Californy, you can go there."

Meanwhile Marlowe's attention had been drawn to the coat. It struck him that he had seen it before. He soon remembered. Surely it was the one that he had seen purchased on Chatham Street the same afternoon. Coats in general are not easily distinguishable, but he had noticed a small round spot on the lapel of that, and the same reappeared on the coat which Julius brought home.

CHAPTER XV

SUSPICION

Julius had been about the streets all day, and felt tired. He threw himself down in the corner, and was soon asleep. Marlowe and Jack kept on with their game, the latter wholly unconscious of the thoughts that were passing through the mind of his companion.

Finally Marlowe, at the conclusion of a game, said: "I won't play any more tonight, Jack."

"Tired, eh?"

"Tired of playing, but I've got something to say to you."

"Out with it," said Morgan, tilting his chair back against the wall.

"Wait a minute."

Saying this, Marlowe rose from his seat, and advancing to the corner, leaned over the sleeping boy, and listened intently to his deep regular breathing.

"What's up?" asked Morgan, surprised.

"I wanted to make sure that the boy was asleep," answered Marlowe.

"Why? Don't you want him to hear?"

"No, I don't; for what I have to say is about him."

"Go ahead."

"I mistrust that he's going to sell us, Jack."

"What!" exclaimed Morgan.

"Don't speak so loud. You might wake him."

As he spoke, Marlowe came back and resumed his seat, bending over and speaking to Jack in a low tone.

"What have you got into your head, Marlowe?" said Jack incredulously. "Julius sell us! Impossible!"

"Why impossible?"

"He'd never think of such a thing. What put it into your head?"

"I'll tell you. Do you see that coat he brought home?"

"Yes. What of it?"

"The boy—Paul Hoffman—gave it to him. I saw him buy it this afternoon in a secondhand store on Chatham Street."

"Are you sure the coat is the same?"

"Yes; I know it by a spot I noticed at the time. Now, what should he take the trouble to buy a coat for unless the boy had done him some service? It's different from giving him an old coat he had thrown aside."

"That's so," said Jack thoughtfully. "Perhaps he's took a fancy to Julius."

"Perhaps he has," repeated Marlowe incredulously. "You know he ain't rich enough to buy coats to give away."

"I can't think the boy would betray us," said Jack slowly.

"Perhaps he wouldn't; I ain't sure; but we must guard against it."

"How?

"We must attack the house sooner than we meant. Suppose we say Saturday night?"

"The boy will be in the house."

"It can't be helped. If he makes trouble we must silence him."

"I'd rather have a clear field Monday night."

"So would I; but suppose the cops are waiting for us?"

"If I thought Julius would do that," said Jack, scowling at the sleeping boy, "I'd kill him myself."

"I don't see why we can't do it Saturday night. We can easily overpower young Hoffman. As for Julius, he'll be asleep. Of course, he mustn't know of our change of plan."

"If you think it best," said Morgan in a tone of indecision; "but I'm almost sure I can trust the boy."

"I trust nobody," said Marlowe. "I wouldn't trust my own brother, if he had an interest in goin' against me."

"Do you trust me?" asked Jack, smiling.

"Yes, I trust you, for we are both in the same boat. It wouldn't do you any good to betray me."

"Yes, we're both in the same boat, but you're steerin'. Well, Marlowe, just make your plans, and count me in. You always had a better headpiece than I."

"Then Saturday night let it be. Today's Thursday."

"Then we have only two days to get ready."

"It will do."

"We'll lock the boy in that night, so he can't make mischief if he wakes up and finds that we are gone."

During this conversation Julius remained fast asleep. Jack soon lay down, and Marlowe also, the latter having taken up his quarters with his friend. The next morning Julius was the first to wake. He leaned on his elbow and looked carelessly at the sleepers. Big, bloated, with a coarse, ruffianly face, Jack lay back with his mouth open, anything but a sleeping beauty. Julius had never thought much of his appearance, but now that he had himself begun to cherish some faint aspirations to elevate himself above his present condition, he looked upon his associates with different eyes, and it struck him forcibly that his guardian had a decidedly disreputable look.

"I won't stay with him long," thought Julius. "If he's took by the cops, I'll set up for myself and never go back to him."

Marlowe lay alongside of his companion, not so disreputable as he in appearance, but not a whit better as regards character. He was the abler of the two mentally, and so was the more dangerous. As Julius looked at him carelessly, he was startled to hear Marlowe talk in his sleep. He was prompted by a natural curiosity to listen, and this was what he heard:

"Don't trust the boy! Make it Saturday night."

These words fastened the attention of Julius. His heart beat quicker as it was revealed to him that his want of fidelity was discovered, or at least suspected. He lay quite still, hoping to hear more. But Marlowe said nothing in addition. Indeed, these words were the precursor of his waking.

Julius saw the indications of this, and prudently closed his own eyes and counterfeited sleep. So when Marlowe in turn looked about him he saw, as he thought, that both his companions were asleep. He did not get up, for there was nothing to call him up early. He was not one of the toiling thousands who are interested in the passage of eight-hour laws. Eight hours of honest industry would not have been to his taste. He turned over, but did not again fall asleep.

Meanwhile Julius, after a sufficient interval, appeared to wake up. He rose from his couch, and gave himself a general shake. This was his way of making his morning toilet.

"Are you awake, Julius?" asked Marlowe.

"Yes."

"You sleep sound don't you?"

"Like a top."

"How did they treat you at that house on Madison Avenue?"

"They was kind to me. They gave me some dinner."

"Did they ask you if you had a father?"

"Yes."

"What did you tell 'em?"

"That I hadn't got none."

"Did they ask who you lived with?"

"Yes," said Julius, after a slight pause.

"And you told 'em?"

"I told 'em I lived with a friend some of the time, when he wasn't absent in the country," said Julius, grinning, as he referred to Jack's frequent terms of enforced seclusion.

"Was you ever at the Island, Julius?"

"No."

"That's odd! You don't do credit to Jack's teaching."

"Likely I'll go some time," said Julius, who, knowing that he was suspected, thought it would not do to seem too virtuous.

"It ain't so bad when you're used to it. Let me see that coat."

Julius tossed it over to Marlowe. It was the only part of his clothing which he had taken off when he went to bed.

"It's a good coat."

"Yes, a bully one."

"The boy—young Hoffman—used to wear it, didn't he?"

"Likely he did, but he's a good deal too big to wear it now."

"How big is he?"

"Most as tall as Jack," said Julius, Jack being considerably shorter than Marlowe.

"Big enough to make trouble. However, he'll get a telegram Monday, to go over to Brooklyn, that'll get him out of the way."

"That's a good plan, that is!" said Julius, knowing very well that it was only said to deceive him.

"Shall you see him today?"

"If you want me to."

"I don't know," said Marlowe. "Do you know where he sleeps?"

"No," said Julius. "You didn't tell me to ask."

"Of course not. It would only make him suspect something. But I didn't know but you heard something said, as you did about the safe."

He eyed Julius keenly as he spoke, and the boy perceiving it, concluded that this was the cause of the sudden suspicion which appeared to have been formed in Marlowe's mind. Of course he

---

knew nothing of the coat, as Paul had not told him of having purchased it.

"I didn't hear nothin' said about it," he answered. "If he's away, you won't mind."

"That's true. I suppose you didn't find out where his mother sleeps."

"Yes, I did. It's the front basement. There was a bed in the room."

Marlowe asked no further questions, and the conversation dropped. Julius threw his blacking-box over his back, and opening the door went out. His mind was busily occupied with the revelation which he had unexpectedly overhead. It seemed clear that the plans of the burglars had been changed, and that the attack was to be made on Saturday night, and not on Monday night, as first proposed. He must tell Paul Hoffman, for he had made his choice between his new friend and his old guardian. On the one side was respectability; on the other a disreputable life, and Julius had seen enough of what it had brought to Jack not to relish the prospect in his own case. He determined to acquaint Paul with the change of plan, and went around to Broadway for that purpose. But Paul had not got opened for business. He had delayed in order to do an errand for his mother.

"I can go later," thought Julius. "It will do just as well."

In this he was mistaken, as we shall see.

CHAPTER XVI

LOCKED UP FOR THE NIGHT

About nine o'clock, after a comfortable breakfast, for which he had paid out of his morning's earnings, Julius went round again to Paul's necktie stand. He had just opened for business when the boy came up.

"You're late this mornin'," said Julius. "I was here before."

"Yes; I was detained at home. Is there anything new?"

"Yes, there is," said Julius.

"What is it?"

"They suspect somethin'."

"Who?"

"Jack and Marlowe. They think I ain't to be trusted."

"How do you know? Did they tell you so?" inquired Paul, with interest.

"No; Marlowe talked in his sleep."

"What did he say?"

"Don't trust the boy! Make it Saturday night."

"Saturday night!" repeated Paul in excitement. "Why, that's tomorrow night."

Julius nodded.

"Do they know you overheard?"

"No."

"So you came and told me. You're a good fellow, Julius. You have done me a great favor."

"You've been good to me," said Julius. "That's why I did it."

"I shall be ready for them tomorrow night, then," said Paul.

This conference was watched, though neither Julius nor Paul was aware of it. Marlowe, on leaving the room some time after Julius, had come into the vicinity with the design of getting a view of Paul and ascertaining whether he was the boy whom he had seen purchasing the coat. He came up a moment after Julius reached the stand. Of course he identified Paul, and his suspicions as to the good understanding between him and Julius were confirmed by seeing them together. He listened intently, hoping to catch something of their conversation, but though not far off, the street noises were such as to render this impossible.

"The young viper!" he said to himself. "He's sold us, as sure as my name's Marlowe. I'll wring his neck for him. He'll find he's got into dangerous business."

He went back and reported to Jack what he had seen.

"If I thought the boy was playin' us a trick," growled Jack, "I'd strangle him; but I ain't sure. You didn't hear what he said?"

"No; I couldn't hear, but it stands to reason that he's sold us."

"What do you want me to do?"

"Nothing yet. The boy don't know that we have changed our plans. He thinks we trust him. Let him think so, and when we get ready to go out Saturday night, we'll tie him hand and foot, so he can't stir. Then we'll go up to the house and take 'em unprepared."

"All right," said Jack. "Your head's longer than mine, Marlowe. You know best."

"Of course I do," said Marlowe. "You've got the strength and I've got the brain."

Jack Morgan extended his arms, and watched his muscular development with satisfaction. He was not sensitive about the slight to his understanding. He was content to be thought what he was, a strong and dangerous animal.

What preparations were necessary to be made were made during that day and the next by the two confederates. They were made during the absence of Julius, that he might know nothing of what was going on. Further to mislead him, the two spoke two or three times on the previous evening of their expedition of Monday night. Julius fathomed their design, and was sharp enough not to appear particularly interested.

So Saturday night came. At six o'clock Julius entered the room and found the two seated together. He had had half a mind not to appear at all, but to cut loose from them forever; but this would lead to suspicion, and he changed his mind. Though he had not seen Paul since, he had reason to believe that he had made preparations to receive the two burglars. In all probability they would be arrested, and this would be their last meeting.

"How are you, Jack?" he said, as he entered the room, with a little qualm at the thought that this man, bad as he was, was so near falling into the hands of justice, and by his means.

Jack looked at him, but did not answer. His expression was menacing, as Julius perceived, and his heart beat more quickly, as he thought, "Has he found out anything?"

85

But luckily for him neither Jack nor Marlowe knew anything definite. Had it been so, the boy's life would have been in peril.

"Have you seen young Hoffman today?" asked Marlowe.

"No."

"He don't know we're going to call Monday night, does he?"

"No," said Julius, and he answered truly. "Where could he find out?"

"You might say something to let him know."

"What would make me do that?" said Julius boldly.

"You might think he'd pay you for telling him."

"He ain't rich," said Julius.

"Do you know what I'd do to you if I found out as you'd sold us," here broke in Jack Morgan, his dull eyes gleaming fiercely. "I'd kill you."

"What makes you say that to me, Jack?" said Julius, not showing the fear he felt.

"Oh, it ain't nothin' to you, then?"

"No, it isn't."

Of course this was a falsehood, but it would have been idle to expect the truth from one like Julius, under such circumstances. He knew Jack well enough to understand that he was quite capable of carrying out his threat, and it decided him, when the two went out, to go out himself and not to return. They might find out that he had been dealing falsely with them, and if so his life was in danger. It was yet early, and he decided to go out at once, as he usually did, for it was not very agreeable to pass an entire evening in the miserable tenement rooms.

"Where are you going?" asked Marlowe, as he lifted the latch of the door.

"I'm goin' out. I haven't had any dinner."

"You can do without dinner tonight, eh, Jack?"

"Yes, he can do without dinner tonight."

"Why? What's up?" demanded the boy.

"Never mind what's up," answered Marlowe. "You ain't goin' out tonight."

"I'm hungry."

"We'll bring you some dinner. We're goin' out ourselves."

"You never kept me in before," said Julius, who felt that it was best to show surprise at the action of the confederates, though it did not surprise him.

"That's neither here nor there. You ain't goin' out tonight."

"All right," said Julius, "if you say so; only bring a feller some grub."

"We'll bring you some," said Jack, who was not as fully convinced as his comrade of Julius' treachery.

They left the room, carefully locking the door behind them.

Julius sat down on the bed, and began to review the situation. Evidently he was to be locked up in the room through the night, while Jack and Marlowe were robbing the house on Madison Avenue. In all probability they would be arrested, and prevented from returning. But suppose one or both escaped from the trap in which they were expected to fall. If their suspicions of his fidelity were aroused now they would be confirmed by the discovery of the police. Knowing the desperate character of both, Julius reflected with a shudder that his life would possibly be sacrificed. It would not do for him to remain here. He must escape by some means.

But how? This was a difficult question to answer. The room was on the third floor, with a solitary window looking out into a small, dirty court. It was too high up to jump with safety, and there was nothing in the room by which he could descend.

He was still considering this question an hour later, when the two returned.

Jack had in his hand a couple of apples.

"There," said he, tossing them to Julius. "That'll do you till mornin'."

"Thank you," said Julius.

It was true that he had had no dinner, and he ate the apples with a good appetite. The two men sat down, and, producing the same old, greasy pack of cards which they had before used, began to play. It was not until a late hour that they could go about the business which they had planned. Twelve o'clock was as early as they could venture to attempt entering the house. To prime them for the task, they had brought in with them a plentiful supply of whisky, of which they partook at frequent intervals. They offered none to Julius.

By and by Julius went to bed. He knew they would not go out till eleven, probably, and he would like to have kept awake till then. But this would have been unusual, and perhaps have increased suspicion. So after a while he lay quiet, and pretended to be asleep. The men kept on playing cards till half-past ten. Then Marlowe spoke:

"We'll hold up now. It's time to be goin'."

"What time is it?"

"Most eleven."

"The boy's asleep."

"Is he?"

Marlowe went to the bed and leaned over. Julius felt his breath on his face, but gave no sign that he was still awake. He was filled with curiosity to know whether Marlowe and Jack meant to carry out their plan this evening.

"He seems to be asleep," said Marlowe, "but we'll lock him in, to make sure. In three hours we'll be back, if all goes well, with plenty of swag."

"I hope so, Marlowe. I've got tired of livin' this way; we'll go to California if we come out right."

"I'm with you, Jack, on that. A pal of mine went out to the mines and got rich. Then he swore off and turned respectable."

"So would I, if I had plenty of tin."

"I've no objection myself, with plenty of money to back me. Money's what makes the difference between people in this world. Give me a hundred thousand, and instead of bein' Tom Marlowe I would be Thomas Marlowe, Esq., our eminent fellow-citizen, and you would be the Hon. John Morgan, eh, Jack?"

Jack laughed at the unfamiliar title, though possibly he was no more undeserving of it than some who flaunt it in the face of society.

"I'm the figger for an Honorable," he said. "But it's time to be goin'. Here's good luck!" and he poured down a glass of the whisky at one gulp.

They carefully locked the door behind them, and their heavy steps were heard descending the rickety stairs.

Julius listened till the sound was no longer heard. Then he jumped up from the pallet on which he had been counterfeiting sleep, and said to himself, "It ain't safe to stay here any longer. How shall I get out?"

CHAPTER XVII

TRAPPED

It was close upon midnight when Marlowe and Jack approached the house on Madison Avenue. There was one thing connected with the position of the house, not before mentioned, which favored their attempt. It was a corner house, and in the rear a high wall separated the area from the street. The two confederates judged that this would be the most feasible way of entrance.

"Boost me up, Marlowe, first," said Jack Morgan. "You're lighter'n me, and can get up alone. I'm fat and clumsy, and I couldn't 'go it alone' to save my neck."

"All right, Jack. Are you ready?"

"Yes. Shove away."

Jack, raised by his companion, got firm hold of the top of the wall, and by an effort clambered over.

"I'm over, all right," he said, in a low voice. "Get over yourself."

Marlowe looked cautiously up and down the street, till he was satisfied no policeman was in sight, then, making a leap, seized the wall, and, by the exercise of his strength, drew himself up, and then, of course, easily descended into the area.

"Here we are," said Jack, in a tone of satisfaction. "Now for work."

"The lights are all out," said Marlowe, softly. "I hope they are all asleep."

"It's likely they are."

"Did Julius say whether any of them slept in the basement?"

"He didn't find out."

"Well, we must risk it. We'll reconnoiter a little and see what's the best way to get in."

At length it was decided that a particular window afforded the easiest ingress. Of course it was fastened inside; but they were not novices, and this presented not the slightest difficulty to their practiced hands. With an instrument pointed with a diamond, they cut out the pane of glass just beneath, and, thrusting in a hand, Marlowe turned back the fastening. Then the window was softly raised, and both entered.

—

They were now in the kitchen. It was dangerous to grope about in the dark, for some article of furniture might be overturned, and that would probably create an alarm which would be fatal to their plans. The first thing, therefore, was to strike a light.

They had a dark lantern with them, and this was speedily lighted. Then both removed their shoes, and one after the other filed into the entry.

"Take care, Jack," said Marlowe. "The woman may be sleeping in the front basement, and might hear you if you make the least noise."

"Suppose she does?"

"We must gag her. If it's the boy, I'll dispose of him pretty quick."

All was still as death. Neither had the slightest idea that their plan was known, and that preparations of a most unwelcome character had been made for their reception—that, in fact, they had ventured into a trap. But on the previous evening Paul had called at the nearest police station, and, communicating what he knew in regard to the intended attack, had asked for a guard. One of the force had been instructed to go back with him and carefully examine the house, the better to provide, not only for defense, but for the capture of the burglars.

"They will enter through the back area window," said the officer at once. "Where do you sleep?"

"My mother and little brother sleep in the front basement. I sleep upstairs."

"The basement must be left vacant."

"Certainly. I wouldn't trust mother and Jimmy there such a night."

"You had better all go upstairs—to the upper floor, if you like—and we will conceal ourselves on the second floor."

"We will do as you think best. I will stay with you."

"No, Paul," said Mrs. Hoffman, terrified.

"I can't think of your exposing yourself to so much danger."

"I'm not afraid, mother. I think it is my duty."

"You can do no good," said the officer. "There will be enough of us to take care of them."

With some reluctance Paul gave up his plan. He was bold and courageous, and, like most boys of his age, he was fond of adventure. An encounter with burglars promised no little excitement, and he wanted to be present, and have his share in it. But when he saw how uneasy and alarmed his mother was, he yielded his desire, as I am sure you, my boy reader, would have done in his place, even had your wish been as strong as his.

Jimmy was now fast asleep; but neither Mrs. Hoffman nor Paul could so readily compose themselves to slumber under the circumstances. They were standing at the head of the attic stairs, listening intently for the slightest sound from below which might indicate the arrival of the expected visitors. At length they heard a pistol shot, then a shriek, then confused noises of feet and voices, and they knew that the encounter had taken place. We must go back and explain what had happened. Carrying their shoes in their hands, the two burglars crept up the basement stairs. Their hopes were high. Their entrance had not yet been observed, and even if it were, they were two strong men against a woman and two boys, the oldest only half-grown. There seemed nothing to fear.

"Now for the safe," said Marlowe. "It's somewhere on the second floor."

"The door of the room may be locked."

"Then it'll take us longer, that's all."

But the door was not locked, and the safe was in the front room on the second floor. In the back room the police were concealed, and were listening intently to the movements of the burglars. Should the latter discover them they were ready for an immediate attack, but they hoped the visitors would get to work first. In this hope they were gratified.

By chance the two confederates entered the front room first.

"Here's the safe, Marlowe," whispered Jack, in tones of satisfaction. "Now, if luck's on our side, we'll make a raise."

"You talk too much," cautioned his companion. "Work first, and talk afterward."

They approached the safe, and Jack kneeled down before it and prepared to effect an entrance. Marlowe was about to follow his example, when his ear, made acute by necessity, distinguished a footstep outside.

"Jack," said he in a sharp whisper, "I hear a step outside."

Instantly Jack Morgan was on his feet.

"Do you think we are heard?"

"Perhaps so. If we are we must secure ourselves. It may be the boy. If it is, we'll quiet him pretty quickly."

They never dreamed of any opposition which they would be unable to withstand. Paul was, of course, no match for them, and as to Mrs. Hoffman, she might go into a fit of hysterics, or might give the alarm. It would be easy to dispose of her. Since, therefore, there was nothing to fear, the two confederates thought it best to face the enemy at once and put him hors de combat.

Thereupon Marlowe opened the door at once, and, to his dismay, found himself confronted by four stalwart policemen.

"The game's up, Jack!" he shouted. "Save yourself!"

He made a spring, eluding the grasp of the officers, and plunged downstairs at a breakneck rate. Meanwhile Jack had snapped a pistol at one of the policemen, but it missed fire. By a return shot he was wounded in the shoulder, and his right arm hung useless. He broke into a volley of execrations.

"Do you surrender?" demanded the officer, at whom he had fired.

"I must," said Jack, in a surly tone. "You're four to one."

Only one policeman had followed Marlowe downstairs. Circumstances favored the escape of this, the more dangerous villain of the two. At the foot of the basement stairs was a door, and on the outside was a bolt. This Marlowe had noticed on going up, and the knowledge stood him in good stead. He got downstairs sufficiently in advance of the policeman to bolt the door and so obstruct his progress. This gave him time, and time was all-important to him. While the officer was kicking at the door and trying to burst it open, as he finally did, Marlowe dashed through the kitchen and got out at the open window. Then he had to scale the wall; but this was easy to do on the inside, for there was a narrow ledge midway. In less than a minute he was on the pavement outside, and fleeing from the danger under cover of the darkness.

When he had got far enough to dare to slacken his pace time also came for thought, and he was able to consider how it happened that four officers were concealed in the house. There was but one possible explanation.

"It was that cursed boy!" he muttered, grinding his teeth in a fierce rage. "He betrayed us. He upset the likeliest plan I've joined in for years. He shall suffer for it, curse it! Before I go to sleep this night I'll give him a lesson. He won't need but one."

His soul thirsting for revenge, he hurried back to the miserable room in which Julius was confined. He had no doubt of finding him, for he was satisfied the boy could not get out.

Meanwhile Jack Morgan was compelled, by superior force, to surrender at discretion. The blood was trickling from the wound in his shoulder, and on the whole, he looked the burglar to perfection. While they were slipping on the handcuffs the officer who had pursued Marlowe returned and reported that he had escaped.

"Bully for him!" said Jack. "He's smart, Marlowe is!"

"So his name is Marlowe, is it?"

"You knew it before," said Jack, in a surly tone. "Who told you about our coming here tonight?"

"Never mind!" said the officer. "It was our business to find out, and we found out."

"I know well enough who blabbed," growled Jack. "Curse him! I'd like to strangle him."

"I don't know whom you suspect, my man," said the officer; "but I think it'll be some time before you'll have a chance to carry out your benevolent purpose."

"Perhaps it will," returned Jack; "but Marlowe ain't took yet. He'll attend to the business for both of us;" and there was a look of malignant joy on his face as he thought of the sure retribution that would overtake Julius.

CHAPTER XVIII

THE VALUE OF A CLOTHES-LINE

When Julius found himself alone and understood that his companions had actually started on their illegal expedition, he felt that there was pressing need of action. He must escape by some means. While the prospect was that they would be captured, and so prevented from returning, on the other hand, one or both might escape, and in that case he knew enough of their savage and brutal character to realize that he would be in the greatest danger. He rose from his bed, and began to devise ways and means of escape.

The first and most obvious outlet, of course, was the door. But this was locked, and the key was in Marlowe's possession. Then there was the solitary window. It was on the third floor, and looked out into a court. It was too high to jump from, and the only other way was by a rope, but there was no rope in the room. Had there been a bedstead of the right kind, the bedcord would have served his purpose, but there was no bedstead at all. With a democratic contempt for such a luxury, all three slept on the floor. The prospect was not encouraging.

"I wonder if I could hang out of the window?" thought Julius.

He looked out, and decided that he would run the risk of breaking a limb if he attempted it. So that plan had to be given up.

Julius sat down and reflected. It occurred to him that perhaps Mrs. O'Connor's key (she roomed just beneath) would open the door. At any rate it was worth trying.

He stamped on the floor with such force that, as he expected, it attracted the attention of those beneath. Listening intently, he heard the woman ascending the staircase. He began to jump up and down with renewed vigor.

"What's the matter wid ye?" called Mrs. O'Connor through the keyhole. "Are you drunk?"

"I'm sick," returned Julius.

"Is it the jumpin' toothache ye have?" asked the Irish woman.

"I'm awful sick. I don't know what it is."

"Open the door, and I'll come in."

"I can't. The door's locked, and Jack has gone away."

Here Julius began to groan again.

"Poor bye!" said the compassionate woman. "What will I do for ye?"

"Try the door with your key. Perhaps it will open it."

"I'll do that same."

She drew out a key, and tried to put it in the lock, but to no purpose. It would not fit.

"I can't open it," she said.

This was a severe disappointment to Julius, who saw his chances of success fade away one by one.

"Have you got a clothes-line, Mrs. O'Connor?" he asked, suddenly.

"Yes," said the good woman, rather astonished, with a vague idea that Julius expected to cure himself by means of it. "And what for do you want it?"

"If you will go down to the court and throw it up to me, I'll get out of the window."

"And what good will that do you?"

"I will go for the doctor."

"I'll go meself, and save you the trouble."

"But he can't get through the keyhole."

"Thrue for you. Wait a bit, and I'll do it."

Mrs. O'Connor descended, and, obtaining from her room a well-worn clothes-line, went below, and, after two or three futile attempts, succeeded in throwing it up so that Julius could seize it.

"Thank you, Mrs. O'Connor," said the boy in exultation. "I'll come down directly."

He soon had it secured, and then boldly got out of the window and swung off. In a minute he was by the side of his friend.

"How do ye feel now?" asked the good woman, in a tone of sympathy.

"Better," said Julius.

"What made them lock ye up?"

"They didn't think I'd want to go out till mornin'. Good-bye, Mrs. O'Connor; I'm goin' for the doctor. You can get your line in the mornin'."

He left the house with a quick, alert step, showing no further evidence of pain. Mrs. O'Connor noticed it, and wondered that he should have got over his sickness so soon. Julius had been tempted to take her into his confidence and explain the real state of the case, but in the uncertain issue of the burglary he decided that it would not be best.

"Good-bye, old house!" he said, looking back to it in the indistinct light; "I shall never come back and live here again. I'll go down to the wharves and find a place to sleep the rest of the night."

He turned his steps in the direction of the East River. He found an out-of-the-way corner on one of the piers, where he disposed himself for sleep. It was nothing new to him. Scores of times he had spent the night in similar places, and never found fault with the accommodations. They might be poor, but the best of it was there was nothing to pay, and he must be indeed unreasonable who could complain under such circumstances. He fell asleep, but the shadow of recent events was upon him. He dreamed that Marlowe had him by the throat, and woke up in terror to find a dock-hand shaking him by the shoulder.

"Avast there!" said the man, who had caught some phrases from the sailors; "wake up and pay for your lodgin's."

"All my money's in the bank," said Julius. "I can't get at it till the bank opens."

"Not then, either," said the dock-hand, good-humoredly. "Well, I'll let you off this time. Your wife's expectin' you home."

"Are you sure of that?" said Julius. "I told her I was goin' to a party, and she needn't expect me home till mornin'."

"Well, the party's broke up, and you'd better be going," returned the other, good-naturedly.

Meanwhile let us go back to Marlowe, whom we left hurrying home a little past midnight, intent upon wreaking his vengeance on Julius for his treachery. Had he found the boy it would have gone hard with him. The ruffianly instinct of the burglar was predominant, and he might have killed him in the intensity of his blind rage. But the foresight and prudent caution of Julius defeated his wrathful purpose, and when he reached the shabby room which he called home his intended victim had escaped.

Marlowe did not at once discover the boy's flight. He unlocked the door, but it was dark within, for the window looked out upon an enclosed court, and permitted only a scanty light to enter. Before striking a light he locked the door again and put the key in his pocket. This was to prevent the boy's escape on the one hand, and any outside interference on the other. Then he drew a match from his pocket and lighted a fragment of candle upon the table. This done he turned his eyes toward the bed with stern exultation. But this was quickly turned into angry surprise.

"The boy's gone!" he exclaimed, with an oath. "How could he have got out, with the door locked?"

The open window and the rope hanging from it revealed the method of escape.

Marlowe strode to the window with a feeling of keen disappointment. Was he to be robbed of his revenge, after all? He had depended upon this with certainty, and meant to have it, though he should be arrested the next minute, and he knew that, though he had escaped from the house of his meditated crime, he was still in great peril. Doubtless Julius had given full information to the police of his name and residence, and even now they might be in pursuit of him. He ground his teeth when he thought of this, and clenched his fist in the impotent desire for vengeance.

"If I had him here," he muttered, "I'd crush him as I would a spider," and he stamped angrily upon the floor.

But where could he have got the rope? That was the next question. He knew that there was none in the room, and how one could have been smuggled in with the door locked was something that puzzled him. Julius himself could not very well have brought one in, as on account of its bulk it would have attracted the attention either of Jack Morgan or himself. Perhaps the woman downstairs might know something about it, he reflected, and this led him to go down and knock at Mrs. O'Connor's door.

After a little pause Mrs. O'Connor came to the door and opened it.

"What's wanted?" she asked. Then, recognizing her visitor as one of the lodgers in the room above, she added, "Is it the boy?"

"Yes; where is he?" demanded Marlowe, abruptly.

"It's gone to the doctor he is."

"Gone to the doctor!" repeated Marlowe, mystified. "What do you mean?"

"He was taken sick jist after you wint away, and as he couldn't open the door which was locked, he pounded on the floor. My key wouldn't fit, so he asked me to throw up a clothes-line, which I did, and the poor crayther got out of the winder, and wint for the doctor. He'll be back soon, I'm thinkin'."

"No, he won't," growled Marlowe. "He's a thief and a villain, and he's run away."

"Did I iver hear the likes?" exclaimed Mrs. O'Connor. "Who'd have thought it, shure?"

"I've a good mind to wring your neck, for helping him off," said Marlowe, forgetting in his anger the politeness due to the fair sex.

"Would you, thin?" exclaimed Mrs. O'Connor, incensed. "Then my husband would do the same to you, you brute! I am glad the boy's gone, so I am, and I hope he'll never get into your clutches again, you monster! Tim, wake up there, and defind yer wife from the thafe that's insulted her!"

Before Tim O'Connor aroused from his sleep at his wife's call, Marlowe, with a smothered execration, retreated to his own room, and began to consider his position. He must fly. There was no doubt of that. Remaining in his old haunts, he would, unquestionably, fall into the hands of the police, now probably on his track. He must get away, and that very night. Any delay would be dangerous. He must leave the city and remain in hiding for the present.

While he was making hurried preparations steps were heard on the stairs, and there was a loud knocking on the door.

"Who's there?" demanded Marlowe.

"Open, in the name of the law!" was the reply of the officers, who had tracked him to his lair.

"Wait a minute," said Marlowe.

He rushed to the window and descended swiftly by the same rope which had given Julius deliverance (it had escaped the attention of the officers, on account of the darkness), and while the officers were waiting for the door to be opened he eluded their vigilance and made his escape.

CHAPTER XIX

A CURIOSITY SHOP

Marlowe realized that he had made the city too hot to hold him. The police, with whom he had a more intimate acquaintance than he desired, were already on his track, and it was doubtful if he could escape. The affair in which he was implicated was a serious one, and if arrested and tried he could hardly hope for less than ten years' imprisonment. This is rather a long term of confinement to be taken out of a man's life, and must be avoided if possible. But one way of escape seemed feasible, and this Marlowe tried, as a desperate experiment.

He made his way swiftly through the darkness to a tumble-down building not far from Baxter Street. The front door was unlocked. He opened it, and feeling his way up—for there were no lights— knocked in a peculiar way at a door just at the head of the stairs. His knock was evidently heard, for shuffling steps were heard within, a bolt was drawn, and Marlowe confronted a little old man, of feeble frame and deeply furrowed face, who scanned the face of his visitor by the light of a candle which he held above his head.

"Why, it's Marlowe!" he said.

"Hush, Jacob! Don't mention my name! I'm in trouble."

"What's in the wind now?"

"Shut the door and I'll tell you."

I may as well say that the conversation which ensued was interlarded with expressions common to the lawless class which Marlowe represented, but I prefer to translate them into common speech. The room which they entered seemed full of odds and ends of wearing apparel, and might have been taken for a pawnbroker's shop, or secondhand clothing store. Or it might have been taken for a dressing-room to a theatre, but that the articles displayed had long since seen their best days, with few exceptions.

"What have you been up to?" asked Jacob, varying the form of his question.

"Jack Morgan and I tried to break into a house on Madison Avenue tonight."

"Couldn't you get in?"

"Yes; but the police were in waiting for us. They nabbed Jack, but I got away. They followed me to Jack's room, but I got out of the window. They're on my track now."

"They didn't see you come in here?" asked the old man, alarmed.

"No, I have given them the slip. But they'll have me unless you help me."

"My son, I'll do what I can. What is your plan?"

"To disguise myself so that my own mother wouldn't know me. See what you can do for me."

My reader will now understand the character of the old man's business. Thieves, and others who had rendered themselves amenable to the law, came to him for disguises, paying heavily for the use of what articles he supplied them. In many cases he was obliged to give them credit, but the old adage, "There is honor among thieves," was exemplified here, for he seldom failed, sooner or later, to receive full payment. It might be, and probably was, from motives of policy that his customers were so honorable; for if unfaithful to their agreements they could hardly expect to be accommodated a second time, and this was a serious consideration.

**A clothing shop like the one where Marlowe
got his disguise and slept for the night.**

When appealed to by Marlowe, Jacob understood that the details of the disguise were left to his judgment. He raised his candle, and took a good look at his customer. Then he dove under a heap of clothing on the floor, and fished out a dirty sailor's dress. "Try it on," he said.

"I don't know about that," said Marlowe, hesitating. "I don't know any sailor's lingo."

"That's no matter. You can say, 'shiver my timbers,' can't you?"

"Yes, I can do that."

"That's enough. It's all I know myself. But it won't do any harm to pick up something else; the police won't never think of you as a sailor."

"I don't know but you're right, Jacob, shiver my timbers if I don't!" and he laughed as he used the expression.

"Try it on. I guess it'll be about right," said the old man.

Marlowe quickly stripped off the suit he wore, and arrayed himself in the strange and unfamiliar garb presented. By good luck it had originally been made for a man of about his size, and there was no discrepancy likely to excite suspicion.

"Let me look at myself," said he.

Jacob produced a small cracked glass, and the ex-burglar surveyed his transformed figure.

"What do you think of it?" asked the dealer.

"The dress is well enough, but they'll know my face."

"Sit down."

"What for?"

"I must cut your hair."

"What then?"

"I'll give you a red wig. There's nothing will disguise you so quick as different colored hair."

"Have you got a wig?"

"Yes, here it is."

"It's ugly enough."

"Better wear it than your own hair at Sing Sing."

"That's where you're right, old man! Go ahead. You understand your business. I'll put myself in your hands."

Marlowe sat down in a wooden chair with a broken back, and the old man proceeded, with trembling hands, to cut his black locks with a pair of large shears, which he kept for this and other purposes.

"You're cutting it pretty close, Jacob. I shall look like a scarecrow."

"All the better," said the old man, laconically.

When the operation was over, Marlowe surveyed his closely-cropped head in the cracked mirror with some disgust.

"You've made a beauty of me," he said. "However, it had to be done. Now where's that wig?"

He was adjusting it awkwardly, when Jacob took it from his hands and put it on properly.

"Now look at yourself," he said.

Marlowe did look, and, as the old man had predicted, found his looks so transformed that he hardly knew himself.

"That's good," he said, in a tone of satisfaction. "It don't improve my beauty, but then I ain't vain. I care more for my liberty. If it hadn't been for that cussed boy there wouldn't have been any need of this."

"What boy?"

"Jack Morgan's boy—Julius."

"What did he do?"

"He split on us—gave warning of our attempt. That's how we came to be taken. I'd give something to get at him."

"Maybe you will."

"I'll try, at any rate. If not now, my revenge will keep. Is that all?"

"Not quite. Sit down again."

The old man stained the face of his visitor so adroitly that he appeared to be deeply pitted with smallpox.

"Your own mother wouldn't know you now," he said with pride.

"That's so, Jacob! You're a regular genius," replied Marlowe. "I ain't sure about it's being me. You're sure about it?"

"Shiver your timbers!" said the old man.

"Shiver my timbers, but I forgot about it! Do you think I'll do?"

"Yes; but you mustn't wash your face till it is dry."

"I sometimes forget to do it now. I guess I can get along without it for a day or two. Now, how much are you going to ask for all this?"

"Seventy-five dollars."

"It's a good deal."

"How long would you get if you got took?" asked Jacob, significantly.

"You're right. It's worth the money. But I can't pay you now, Jacob."

"You won't forget it," said the old man, composedly, for he expected this, since Marlowe's attempt at burglary had been unsuccessful. "You'll pay me when you can."

"Shiver my timbers, messmate, but I will!"

"Good!" said the old man. "You're getting it."

"I don't think those landlubbers—the cops—will know me in this rig-out."

"Better. You'll do."

"Well, Jacob, I'll pay you as soon as I can. By the way, haven't you any place where you can stow me for the night? It won't do for me to go back to Jack's room; it's too hot for me."

"Lay down anywhere," said Jacob. "I haven't got any bed; I lie down on the clothes."

"That'll do; I ain't used to bridal-chambers or silk counterpanes. I am as tired as a dog. Here goes!"

He flung himself down in a corner on an indiscriminate pile of clothing, and in five minutes was breathing deeply, and fast asleep. Had he been a novice in his illegal profession, the two narrow escapes he had just had, and the risk which, in spite of his disguise he at present run, would have excited him and prevented his sleeping; but he was an old hand and used to danger. It was not the first time he had eluded the authorities, and was not likely to be the last, so he fell asleep upon his strange couch, and slept as unconcernedly as an infant. The old man did not immediately lie down. He held up and examined attentively the suit Marlowe had thrown oft, which, according to custom, became his perquisite, in addition to the cash payment demanded, and was gratified to find it in good condition. He next plunged his hands into the pockets, but Marlowe had transferred their contents to his new attire. However, Jacob would have been little richer had his visitor neglected to do so. Having finished his scrutiny the old man blew out the candle and lay down in the corner opposite Marlowe.

CHAPTER XX

THE DISGUISED LISTENER

On the Monday morning succeeding the attempt at burglary so happily defeated, Paul thought he ought to go round to the counting-room of Mr. Preston and acquaint him with the particulars. He accordingly deferred opening his place of business—if I may use so ambitious a phrase of the humble necktie stand over which he presided—and bent his steps toward Mr. Preston's counting-room. The latter had just arrived.

"Good-morning, Paul," said Mr. Preston, smiling. "I know all about it."

"About what, sir?" inquired Paul, surprised.

"About the burglary."

"Who told you?" our hero asked, in astonishment.

"Didn't you know it was in the papers?"

"No, sir."

"I read it on my way downtown. These reporters get hold of everything. Read that."

Mr. Preston put into Paul's hands a morning paper, pointing to the following paragraph:

"On Saturday evening an attempt was made to rob the house of Nathaniel Talbot, No. — Madison Avenue. The attempt was made by two well-known burglars, familiarly known as Jack Morgan and Tom Marlowe. The enterprise promised to be successful, as Mr. Talbot is absent in Europe with his family. During his absence the house is taken care of by a Mrs. Hoffman, whose son Paul, a boy of sixteen, keeps a necktie stand below the Astor House. Paul, who seems to be possessed of courage and coolness, learned that the attempt was about to be made, and determined not only to frustrate it, but to get hold of the burglars. He gave information at police headquarters, and when the brace of worthies arrived they met a reception as unexpected as it was unwelcome. They were permitted to effect an entrance, and met with no drawback till they reached the second story. Then the police made their appearance on the scene and effected the capture of Morgan. Marlowe succeeded in effecting his escape, but the police are on his track, and his haunts in the city being known, there is every reason to believe that he will be captured. Great credit is due to the boy Paul, through whose bravery and good judgment Mr. Talbot's house has been saved from robbery, and probably two noted desperadoes captured."

Paul read this paragraph with pleasure, as may readily be supposed. He was glad to find that his efforts on Mr. Talbot's behalf were likely to secure recognition.

"I never thought of getting into the papers," he said, looking up. "I don't see how the reporters found out about it."

"Oh, the reporters are everywhere. Probably they call every evening at police quarters and obtain information of all such cases. You see, Paul, you are getting famous."

"I only did what I ought to do," said Paul, modestly.

"I agree to that, but that is more than many of us can say. If we all could say it with justice, we should have a very different world from what we have at present."

"Besides," said Paul, who, though he liked praise, wanted to be just, "there is some one else, a boy, too, who had more to do with the affair than I."

"Who was that?"

"The boy who told me the house was to be entered."

"Tell me all about it. I told you I knew all about it, but there is one thing the paper does not explain how you found out the plans of those villains."

"I will tell you, sir. One day I saw a boy in front of the eating-house where I usually dine, who looked hungry. I have known what it was to be hungry myself, and I pitied him. So I asked him in and gave him some lunch. I think it was the next day that he came round and asked me if I did not live in Mr. Talbot's house on Madison Avenue. He said the man he lived with and another were intending to break into it and rob the safe. They seemed to know that my mother and myself were the only ones who occupied it."

"How old a boy was he?"

"I don't know his age. He looks about twelve, but he may be older."

"What do you suppose made him bring you the information?"

"I think he felt grateful for the lunch I gave him."

"Did you see him more than once?"

"Yes, several times. It seems the two men intended at first to make the attempt this evening, but for some reason they came to distrust the boy, who was acquainted with their plans, and fixed it for

Saturday. They didn't intend to let him know of their change of plan, but he overheard one of them talking in his sleep. He came and told me. This was lucky, as otherwise I should not have been ready for them."

"What is the name of this boy?"
"Julius."

"He has certainly done you and Mr. Talbot great service. What is your opinion of him? Has he been spoiled by living with thieves?"

"I don't think he has. If he could have a chance to do better, I think he would."

"He shall have a chance. I suppose you will see him soon."

"I shouldn't wonder if he would come round to my stand today."

"If he does, bring him here."

"Yes, sir, I will."

"What you have told me, Paul," continued Mr. Preston, "does not lessen your own merits. But for your kindness to this poor boy you would have heard nothing of the intended burglary, and been unable to take the measures which have proved so happily successful."

"You are determined to praise me, Mr. Preston," said Paul.

"Because you deserve it. I shall take care to write particulars to Mr. Talbot, who will doubtless have seen the paragraph you have just read, and will be interested to hear more. I shall not forget your part in the affair."

"Thank you, sir. I shall be glad to have Mr. Talbot know that I am faithful to his interests."

"He shall know it."

A boy entered the office at this point, with a number of letters from the post office, and Mr. Preston began to read them. Paul saw that it was time to go, and bade him good-morning.

"Good-morning, Paul," said his patron. "Don't forget to bring me the boy, Julius."

"I won't forget, sir."

Paul was not likely to forget, for he, too, felt grateful to Julius, and was glad to think the poor boy was likely to receive a reward for his services. Through the arrest of Jack Morgan he would be thrown upon his own exertions, and aid would doubtless be welcome. Paul felt an honorable satisfaction in knowing that he was rising in the world, and he was unselfish enough to desire to see others prosper also.

He was not mistaken in supposing Julius would call upon him. About eleven o'clock he came up to the stand.

"Good-morning, Julius," said Paul, cordially.

"Good-morning," said the smaller boy. "Was Jack and Marlowe round to your house Saturday night?"

"Yes."

"Was they took?" asked Julius, anxiously.

"Morgan was captured, but Marlowe escaped."

The boy's countenance fell, and he looked alarmed.

"Do you think they'll take him?"

"They are on his track. I don't think that he can escape."

"If he does he'll kill me," said Julius; "he suspected me afore. Now he'll know I let out about him and Jack."

"He won't dare to come near you."

"Why won't he?"

"He knows the police are after him; he'll hide somewhere."

"I don't know," said Julius, thoughtfully.

"He'll be awful mad with me. He'll try to do me some harm if he can."

"I should be sorry to have any harm come to you, Julius," said Paul, earnestly. "If Marlowe is arrested it will be all right."

"He shut me up last night before he went away; Jack and he did."

"How was that?"

Julius gave an account of his confinement, and how he escaped through the help of Mrs. O'Connor. He did not know of Marlowe's subsequent visit to the room, and his disappointment at finding the bird flown. He did not know of this, not having dared to go round there since, lest he should come upon Jack or Marlowe. Now he knew it was only the latter he had to fear.

"You managed it pretty well about getting away," said Paul. "It reminds me of something that happened to me—I was locked up in a hotel once the same way," and he gave Julius a little account of his adventure at Lovejoy's Hotel, with the jeweler from Syracuse, as narrated in an earlier volume of this series, "Paul the Peddler." Julius was interested in the story.

"Have you got any money, Julius?" asked Paul, when he had finished.

"I've got ten cents. I didn't have much luck this mornin'. I left my blackin'-box in the room, and I didn't dare to go after it, as I thought I might meet Marlowe or Jack."

"Haven't you had any breakfast, then?"

"Yes, I went down to the Long Branch boat and got a chance to carry a carpet-bag. The gentleman gave me a quarter; I spent fifteen cents for breakfast, and I've got ten left."

"You must stop and go to lunch with me, Julius. It is twenty minutes to eleven already. I shall go at twelve."

"You spend too much money on me," said Julius.

"Never mind that. Where would I be if you hadn't told me about this burglary? I should have known nothing about it, and I might have been murdered. I've told about you to Mr. Preston, a friend of Mr. Talbot, whose house I live in, and he wants me to bring you round to his counting-room. He is going to do something for you."

Julius brightened up. He had never had any friend excepting Jack Morgan, and the reader can form some idea of the value of such a friend as Jack.

"When does he want me to come to his room?" he asked.

"I'll go round with you after lunch. You want to rise in the world, don't you, Julius?"

"I'd like to, but I ain't had any chance."

"I think Mr. Preston will give you a chance. You can be thinking what you would like to do, and he will help you to it."

"I would like to go out West. I'm afraid to stay here. Marlowe might find me."

"I don't know but you are right, Julius. Out West there is more of a chance to rise. You can tell Mr. Preston what you wish."

While the boys were talking a man stood nearby, who listened attentively to what was said, hearing every word. Neither Paul nor Julius remarked him. He was a tall man, with red hair, and a face marked by the smallpox. He was dressed in the garb of a sailor. Of course this was Marlowe. It was imprudent for him to post himself in so public a place, but he trusted to his disguise, and he wanted to hear for himself the conversation between the two boys. He learned, what he suspected before, that to the boy, Julius, he was indebted for the failure of his attempt at burglary. When the two boys went to lunch he followed them

CHAPTER XXI

A BRIGHTER PROSPECT FOR JULIUS

After lunch Paul went again to Mr. Preston's place of business, accompanied by Julius. The disguised sailor, who had lingered outside the restaurant, followed the two at a safe distance. Had not Paul and Julius been so occupied with their own affairs, they might have noticed Marlowe. As it was, they were quite unconscious of being followed.

They were fortunate in finding Mr. Preston in his office, and at leisure.

"Mr. Preston," said Paul, "this is the boy I spoke to you about."

"What is your name, my lad?" asked the merchant.

"Julius," answered the street boy.

"My young friend, Paul, tells me that you have done him and his employer a great service. Did you live with the men who were engaged in the burglary?"

"Yes, sir."

"I suppose they have been in prison at different times?"

"Yes, sir, more'n half the time."

"What did you do then?"

"Worked for myself."

"What did you do?"

"Blacked boots or sold papers. When I got a chance I smashed baggage."

"Did you get paid for that?" asked Mr. Preston, with a smile.

"He means carried bundles or carpet-bags," explained Paul.

"I understand. Did these men ever want you to steal, or join them in burglary?"

"Sometimes. They was goin' to take me last night, but they was afraid I'd peach, and locked me up at home."

"I hope you have no desire to become a burglar?"

"No, sir; I want to be respectable, like Paul."

"You are right, there, my lad. Now, have you any plans for the future?"

"I'd like to go out West."

"Would you rather go there than remain in New York?"

"Yes, sir. He's here."

"Who is here?"

"Marlowe. He wasn't took. He'll murder me if he gets hold of me."

"Marlowe is one of the burglars, I suppose?"

"Yes, sir; he's the worst."

"I hope he will be taken. Probably he will find it hard to escape, as the police are on his track. But I don't know but you are right about going out West. Many boys like yourself have been sent out by the Children's Aid Society."

"I know some of 'em," said Julius.

"You will stand a better chance of succeeding there than here. I am willing to help you, if you wish to go out."

Mr. Preston took out his wallet, and drew therefrom a roll of bills.

"Here are fifty dollars," he said.

"For me?" asked Julius, in almost incredulous surprise.

"Yes, for you. I hope you will make a good use of it."

Julius selected a five-dollar bill, which he thrust into his vest pocket, and handed the remainder to Paul.

"Keep it for me, Paul," he said; "I might lose it."

"You have done well," said Mr. Preston, approvingly. "Until you leave the city, it will be best to leave the money in Paul's hands. Now, my lad, I must bid you good-morning, as business claims my attention. Try to lead a good life, and you have my best wishes for your welfare."

He offered his hand, which Julius took shyly.

The two boys went out, and again Marlowe followed them and tried to overhear what they said.

"Don't you feel rich, Julius?" he heard Paul say.

"He was very good to me," said Julius.

"Fifty dollars is a good deal of money for a boy like you."

"Fifty dollars!" said Marlowe to himself. "So the young dog got fifty dollars for selling Jack 'n' me? He thinks he's done a good thing. We'll see! We'll see!"

He instantly conceived the design of getting hold of this fifty dollars. As we know, he was almost penniless, and money he sorely needed to effect his escape from the city, where he was placed in hourly peril. To take it from Julius would give him more pleasure than to obtain it in any other way, for it would be combining revenge with personal profit. Not that this revenge would content him. His resentment was too deep and intense to be satisfied with any such retaliation. He wanted to make the boy suffer. He would hardly have shrunk from taking his life. He was, in fact, a worse man than Jack Morgan, for the latter was not naturally cruel, though, under temptation, he might be led to desperate acts.

"Now tell me what you want to do, Julius," said Paul.

"I want to go out West."

"You are rather young to travel alone. Besides, you don't know anything about the West, do you?"

Julius admitted that he did not. His education had been very much neglected. He probably could not have named half a dozen States, and had the vaguest idea of the West. He had heard it spoken of, and some boys whom he used to know about the streets had gone out there. But beyond that he knew nothing.

"How far do you think it is to the West?" asked Paul.

"About a hundred miles."

"It is all of that," said Paul, laughing. "Now I'll tell you what I would do if I were in your place."

"What?"

"Were you ever in the Newsboys' Lodging House?"

"Lots of times."

"Then you know Mr. O'Connor, the superintendent?"

"Yes; he's very kind to us boys."

"Well, suppose we go round and ask him when the next company of boys starts for the West. You could go with them, and he will find you a place out there. What do you say?"

"I would like to do that," said Julius, with evident satisfaction.

"Then we will go up at once. I guess my business can wait a little longer."

"You're very kind to me," said Julius, gratefully. "You'll lose money goin' round with me so much."

"No matter for that. It won't ruin me. Besides, you've done me a great service. I ought to be willing to do something for you."

"That ain't nothin'."

"I think different. Come along; we'll settle this matter at once."

The Newsboys lodging house in New York.

The two boys kept on their way till they reached the lodging house. All was quiet; for in the day-time the boys are scattered about the streets, earning their livelihood in different ways. Only at dinner-time they come back, and in the evening the rooms are well filled. Paul had been here before, not as a guest, for he had always had a home of his own; but he had called in the evening at different times. Julius had often passed the night there, during the lengthened intervals of Jack's enforced residence in public institutions.

They met Mr. O'Connor just coming out.

"How do you do, Paul? I hope you're well, Julius," said the superintendent, who has a remarkable faculty for remembering the names and faces of the thousands of boys that from time to time frequent the lodging house. "Do you want to see me?"

"Yes, sir," answered Paul; "but we won't detain you long."

"Never mind about that; my business can wait."

"Julius wants to go out West," proceeded Paul. "Now, what we want to find out is, when you are going to send a party out."

"This day week."

"Who is going out with it?"

"It is not quite decided. I may go myself," said the superintendent.

"Can Julius go out with you?"

"Yes; we haven't got our full number. He can go."

"Then you're all right, Julius," said Paul.

"What gave you the idea of going out West, Julius?" asked Mr. O'Connor.

"Marlowe's after me," said Julius, briefly.

The superintendent looked mystified, and Paul explained.

"Didn't you read in the papers," he asked, "about the burglary on Madison Avenue?"

"At Mr. Talbot's house?"

"Yes."

"Had Julius anything to do with that?"

"Through his means the burglars were prevented from carrying out their designs, and one of them was captured. This was Jack Morgan, with whom Julius lived. The other, a man named Marlowe, got off. As he suspected Julius beforehand of betraying them, and is a man of revengeful disposition, Julius is afraid of staying in the city while he is at large. We both think he had better go West. There he may have a chance of doing well."

"No doubt. Why, some of our boys who have gone out there have grown rich. Others have persevered in seeking an education, and there are lawyers, ministers and doctors, as well as merchants, now prosperous and respected, who graduated from the streets of New York, and were sent out by our society."

The face of Julius brightened as he heard these words.

"I hope I'll do well," he said.

"It depends a good deal on yourself, my boy," said the superintendent, kindly. "Firmly resolve to do well, and you will very likely succeed. You've had a rough time of it so far, and circumstances have been against you; but I'll try to find a good place for you, where you'll have a chance to learn something and to improve. Then it will be your own fault if you don't rise to a respectable place in society."

"I'll try," said Julius, hopefully, and he meant what he said. He had lived among social outlaws all his life, and he realized the disadvantages of such a career. He shuddered at the idea of following in the steps of Jack Morgan or Marlowe—a considerable portion of whose time was spent in confinement. He wanted to be like Paul, for whom he felt both respect and attachment, and the superintendent's words encouraged and made him ambitious.

CHAPTER XXII

MARLOWE OVERTAKES HIS VICTIM

On emerging into the street the two boys parted company. It was time for Paul to go back to his business. Julius was more indifferent to employment. He had five dollars in his pocket, and forty-five dollars deposited with Paul. Accustomed to live from hand to mouth, this made him feel very rich. It was a bright, pleasant day, and it occurred to him that it would be very pleasant to make an excursion somewhere, it made little difference to him where. The first place that occurred to him was Staten Island. It is six miles from the city or half an hour by water. The boats start from a pier near the Battery.

"Where's he going, I wonder?" thought Marlowe, following at a little distance.

As no conversation had passed between the boys about the excursion, he was quite in the dark; but he was determined to follow where-ever it might be. He soon ascertained. Julius met a street acquaintance—Tom Barker, a newsboy—and accosted him.

"Tom, come with me."

"Where you goin'?"

"To Staten Island."

"What's up?"

"Nothin'. I'm goin' for the benefit of my health. Come along."

"I can't come."

"Haven't you got the stamps? I'll pay."

"I've got to go to Twenty-seventh Street on an errand. I'll go with you tomorrow."

"Can't wait," said Julius. "I must go alone."

"Goin' to Staten Island," thought Marlowe, in exultation. "I'll get a chance at him there."

Marlowe had not much money with him, but he had enough to pay the fare to Staten Island—ten cents. So he kept on the track of Julius, and passed the wicket just behind him. The boat was approaching the pier, and they had not long to wait. Julius went to the forward part of the boat, and took a seat just in front of the boiler. Marlowe took a position near, but not too near. He had considerable confidence in his disguise, but did not want to run any unnecessary risk of recognition. It so happened that a few steps from him was a genuine specimen of the profession he was counterfeiting. With the sociability characteristic of a sailor, he undertook to open a conversation with Marlowe.

"Hollo, shipmate!" he said.

"Hollo, yourself!" said the counterfeit, not over pleased with the salutation.

"I thought I'd hail you, seein' we both foller the sea. Have you been long ashore?"

"Not long," answered Marlowe.

"Where was your last v'y'ge?"

"To Californy," answered Marlowe, hesitating.

"What craft?"

Here was an embarrassing question. Marlowe wished his questioner at the North Pole, but felt compelled to answer.

"The—Sally Ann," he answered.

"You don't say!" said the other, with animation. "I was aboard the Sally Ann myself, one v'y'ge."

"Confound you, I'm sorry to hear it!" thought the impostor.

"There's more than one Sally Ann, it's likely," he said. "Who was your captain?"

"Captain Rice."

"Mine was Captain Talbot."

"How long was your v'y'ge, shipmate?"

Now Marlowe had no knowledge of the number of days such a voyage ought to take. He knew that the California steamers came in in three or four weeks, and the difference of speed did not occur to him, not to speak of the vastly greater distance round Cape Horn.

"Thirty days," he answered, at random.

"Thirty days!" exclaimed the sailor, in amazement. "Did you go round the Horn in thirty days?"

"Yes, we had favorable winds," explained Marlowe.

"He must be crazy, or he's no sailor," thought the true son of Neptune.

He was about to ask another question, when Marlowe, who suspected that he had made a blunder, turned abruptly, and walked away.

"He ain't no sailor," said the questioner to himself. "He never lived in the forecastle, I know by his walk."

Marlowe had not the rolling gait of a seaman, and the other detected it at once.

"Went round the Horn in thirty days!" soliloquized the sailor. "That yarn's too tough for me to swallow. What's he got on that rig for?"

Meanwhile, Julius looked around him with enjoyment. Cheap as the excursion was, he had but once made it before. It had been seldom that he had even twenty cents to spare, and when he had money, he had preferred to go to the Old Bowery or Tony Pastor's for an evening's entertainment. Now he felt the refreshing influence of the sea breeze. He was safe from Marlowe, so he thought. He had left danger behind him in the great, dusty city. Before him was a vision of green fields, and the delight of an afternoon without work and without care. He was sure of a good dinner and a comfortable bed; for had he not five dollars in his pocket? Julius felt as rich as Stewart or Vanderbilt, and so he was for the time being. But he would have felt anxious, could he have seen the baleful glance of the disguised sailor; for Marlowe, though he had changed his seat, still managed to keep Julius in sight. But there was another who in turn watched him, and that was the genuine sailor. The latter was bent on finding out the meaning of the disguise, for disguise he knew it to be. He was not long in discovering that Marlowe was watching Julius with a malignant glance.

"He hates the lad," thought the sailor. "Does he mean him harm?"

He was making an excursion of pleasure, but he had another object in view. He had a cousin living on Staten Island, and he was intending to make him a call; but this business was not imperative, and he resolved to follow out the present adventure.

"If he tries to harm the lad," said the kindhearted sailor, "he'll have to take me too."

So while Marlowe watched Julius, he was watched in turn.

The boat reached the first landing, and some of the passengers got off. But Julius made no motion to disembark, and of course Marlowe did not. Shortly afterward the second landing was reached; but it was not until the boat touched the third that Julius rose from his seat and descended the stairs to the lower deck. The two sailors followed.

Julius walked up the road that leads to the pier. He had no particular destination. He cared little where he went, his main object being to get back into the country. The sailor soon perceived that Marlowe had no object except to follow Julius. All his movements depended upon the boy's. When Julius turned, he turned also.

"What has he got ag'in the boy?" thought the sailor. "He shan't harm him if Jack Halyard can prevent it."

Marlowe was tall and strong, and a formidable opponent. The sailor was three inches shorter, but he was broad-shouldered, and had an immense chest. It was clear that he was very powerful. He was thoroughly brave also. Fear was a stranger to him, and he did not hesitate for a moment to encounter Marlowe in the boy's defense.

Julius kept on. At one place he stopped to watch two boys who were pitching ball to each other. He asked them if he might join in the game; but the boys looked contemptuously at his shabby clothes, and one of them said, rudely:

"We don't play with ragamuffins."

"I ain't a ragamuffin!" said Julius.

"Perhaps you're a gentleman in disguise," said one, with a sneer.

"I'm as much of a gentleman as you are," retorted Julius, angrily.

"Clear out, you beggar! We don't want you here," said the second boy, arrogantly.

Julius walked on indignantly.

"They insult me because I am poor," he said to himself. "I'll be rich some time, perhaps."

The possibility of becoming rich had never occurred to him before today; but Mr. O'Connor's words, and the fifty dollars which had been given him, made him hopeful and ambitious. He had heard that some of the rich men who owned warehouses in the great city had once been poor boys like himself. Might he not rise like them? For the first time in his life he seemed to be having a chance.

Marlowe saw him leave the boys with satisfaction. Had Julius stopped to play with them his scheme of vengeance would have been delayed, perhaps frustrated. It would not do for him to attack the boy in the presence of others. But Julius was walking away from the village into the interior. If he only went far enough he would be at his mercy.

What should he do to him? He might kill him, but killing is rather a dangerous game to play at in a civilized community.

"I'll take his money," thought Marlowe, "and beat him within an inch of his life. I'll teach him to betray me!"

The Staten Island countryside. This is where Marlowe confronted Julius.

At length Julius wandered to a spot solitary enough to suit his purpose. Strange to say, the boy had not turned, or noticed his pursuer. Marlowe was quite out of his thoughts. Who would think of finding him in this quiet scene? But he was destined to be rudely awakened from his dream of security. All at once he felt a hand upon his shoulder. Turning quickly, he saw one whom he supposed to be a sailor.

"What's wanted?" he asked.

"You're wanted."

"What for?" asked Julius, not yet recognizing his enemy.

"Don't you know me?" asked Marlowe.

"No."

"But I know you, you young villain!" exclaimed Marlowe, unable longer to repress his fury. "I'm the man you sold along with Jack Morgan. I've got a reckoning with you, my lad, and it's goin' to be a heavy one. I haven't followed you all the way from New York for nothing."

CHAPTER XXIII

A TIMELY RESCUE

Julius was filled with a terrible fear, when in the man who stood over him menacingly he recognized Tom Marlowe. He knew the man's brutal disposition, and that he was very much incensed against him. He looked wildly around him for help, but he could see no one. The sailor had hidden behind a large tree, and was not visible.

"You're looking for help, are you?" sneered Marlowe. "Look all you want to. You're in my power. Now tell me, you treacherous young dog, why shouldn't I kill you?"

Julius regarded him in silent terror.

"You didn't think I'd get away from the cops you set on my track, did you? You thought you'd get rid of me, did you? Where's that money you got for selling us, eh?"

"I didn't sell you," said Julius, trembling.

"Don't lie to me. I know all about it. I followed you when you went with that boy that keeps the necktie stand. I know how much you got. It was fifty dollars."

Julius was bewildered. He did not understand how Marlowe could have gained this information.

"Do you deny this?" demanded Marlowe.

"I didn't know I was to get any money," stammered Julius. "I wouldn't have told of you, but Paul had been kind to me."

"So you forgot all about Jack Morgan and me. You were ready to sell your best friends. But you didn't count the cost, my chicken! We generally pay up for such favors. I promised Jack I'd settle our account, and I'm goin' to do it."

"Is Jack took?" asked Julius, shrinking under the man's fierce glance.

"Yes, he is, curse you! If it hadn't been for your blabbing tongue we'd both have got off with the swag. Now hand over that money, and be quick about it."

"What money?" faltered Julius.

"You know well enough—the fifty dollars."

Julius felt thankful now that he had deposited the greater part with Paul.

"I haven't got it."

"You lie!" exclaimed Marlowe, brutally.

"I gave it to Paul, all except five dollars." "I don't believe you. Empty your pockets."

Julius did so, but only five dollars were found. Marlowe was badly disappointed. Fifty dollars would have been of essential service to him, and they had dwindled to five.

"What business had you to give the money to him?" he demanded, harshly.

"I was afraid I might lose it."

"Give me the five dollars."

Julius reluctantly handed the bill to his enemy, who thrust it into his pocket.

"Now," said he, seizing Julius by the shoulder with a dark and menacing look, "I'll give you a lesson you'll remember to the last day of your life."

He threw Julius upon the ground, and was about savagely to kick the helpless boy, who would in all probability have died from the brutal treatment he was likely to receive, when he was seized by the collar, and sent whirling backward by a powerful hand.

"Avast there, you lubber!" said the sailor, who had felt it time to interfere. "What are you about?"

Marlowe turned furiously upon his unexpected assailant.

"I'll soon let you know, if you don't leave here pretty sudden. What business is it of yours?" he said, furiously.

"It's always my business," said the sailor, manfully, "when I see a big brute pitching into a youngster like that. I ain't the man to stand by and see it done."

"He wants to kill me. Don't let him," implored Julius.

"That I won't, my lad. He'll have to kill me, too, if that's what he's after. He'll find me a tough customer, I reckon."

"This is my boy. I shall beat him as I please," said Marlowe, angrily.

"I am not his boy," said Julius, fearing the sailor would credit the statement.

"Don't you be afraid, my lad. If you were his boy ten times over, he shouldn't beat you while I am by."

Marlowe was terribly enraged. He saw his victim slipping from his grasp just as he was about to glut his vengeance upon him. He was a man of violent passions, and they got the better of his prudence.

"Stand back!" he shouted, advancing toward the intrepid sailor, "or I will serve you and the boy alike."

"I'm ready," said the other, coolly, squaring off scientifically.

Marlowe aimed a heavy blow at his head, which, had it taken effect, would have prostrated and perhaps stunned him. But it was warded off, and a counter blow returned, which took better effect. Marlowe staggered under it, but it only maddened him. Half-blinded, he rushed once more upon his opponent, but received a well-directed blow full in the chest, which stretched him at the sailor's feet. The latter forbore to take an unmanly advantage of his foe's position, but calmly waited for him to rise.

"Do you want more?" he asked, coolly.

Marlowe, had he been wise, would have desisted, but he was filled with a blind, unreasoning rage, and advanced again to the attack. But he was no match for the stout sailor. He fared this time no better than before, but again was stretched at the sailor's feet.

By this time the conflict had attracted attention. Several men came running up, among them a member of the local police.

"What's the meaning of all this?" demanded the latter.

"Ask the boy," said the sailor.

Julius, thus appealed to, answered:

"That man wanted to kill me, but the sailor stopped him."

"It's a lie!" growled Marlowe. "He's my boy, and I was punishing him."

"Are you his boy?" asked the policeman, turning to Julius.

"No."

"Where do you live?"

"In New York."

"Do you know him?"

"Yes."

"Who is he?"

Marlowe saw that it was getting dangerous for him, and was anxious to get away.

"The boy may shift for himself," he said. "If you take so much interest in him you can take care of him."

These last words were addressed to the sailor.

He turned on his heel, and hoped to get away without further trouble.

"Stop, there!" said the officer. "We haven't done with you yet."

"What do you want?" demanded Marlowe, endeavoring to conceal his alarm under an air of surly bravado.

"I want to know who you are."

"I'm a sailor."

"Then you're a land sailor," retorted the true son of Neptune.

"Is he a sailor?" asked the officer of Julius.

"No, sir."

"What is his name?"

"His name is Marlowe," answered Julius, in spite of the black and menacing looks of his enemy, intended to intimidate him.

"Marlowe? The man implicated in the burglary on Madison Avenue?"

Julius was not required to answer this, for at the question, showing that he was known, Marlowe with an oath took to flight, closely pursued by all present. He had run half a mile before he was secured. But his pursuers at length caught up with him, and after a sharp struggle, in which they were materially assisted by the powerful sailor, he was taken and bound.

"If I ever get free, I'll kill you!" he muttered, between his teeth, to Julius. "You'll rue this day's work."

Julius, secure as he was at present, could not help shuddering as he heard these threatening words. But he felt thankful that he had escaped the present danger. The peril was over for the time; but Julius could not help feeling that he was not wholly safe as long as Marlowe was at large. I may as well add here that the burglar was delivered to the New York authorities, and in due time had his trial, was convicted and sentenced to ten years' imprisonment in the prison at Sing Sing.

This adventure, and the excitement attending it, spoiled the enjoyment of Julius for the afternoon. He returned to the pier and took passage on the boat bound for the city. He called on Paul at his stand, and surprised him with the news of Marlowe's capture, and his own narrow escape.

Sing Sing prison. Where Jack and Marlowe end up serving time for the break-in at the Talbot house.

"I am glad to hear it, Julius," said Paul. "So that sailor that followed you was Marlowe."

"Yes. Did you see him?"

"I noticed him two or three times, but had no idea he was following us."

"I never should have known him, he looked so different." "He might have got away if he hadn't been so anxious to revenge himself on you."

"He's got my five dollars," said Julius, regretfully.

"It might have been much worse. You've got forty-five dollars left yet. Do you want any of it?"

"You may give me five more."

Paul drew a five-dollar bill from his pocket and handed it to Julius.

"By the way, Julius," he said, "where do you expect to sleep tonight?"

"In the lodgin' house."

"Come up and stop with me. We can find room for you. Besides, my mother will give you a good dinner."

"You are very kind to me, Paul," said Julius, gratefully.

"I ought to be. You did us all a great service. You must stay with us till it is time for you to go out West."

Julius made some faint objections, out of bashfulness; but he was so pleasantly received by Mrs. Hoffman, and treated with so much kindness, that he came to feel quite at home, and needed no urging after the first night. Jimmy asked him a multitude of questions about the burglars, how they looked and how they lived, to which Julius answered patiently.

"When you are out West, you must write to us how you are getting along, Julius," said Mrs. Hoffman, kindly.

Julius blushed, and did not answer. He seemed much embarrassed.

"Won't you?" asked Jimmy.

"I don't know how to write!" said Julius at last, feeling suddenly ashamed of his ignorance.

"Such a big boy as you can't write?" said Jimmy, in amazement.

"There is plenty of time to learn," said Paul, cheerfully. "Julius has had no chance to learn yet, but after he gets to the West he will make it up."

The mortification which Julius felt at his ignorance made him determine to study hard whenever he could. He felt that if he wanted to occupy a respectable position in society, he must, at least, know how to read and write.

CHAPTER XXIV

THE POOR ARTIST

A week later Julius started for the West with a company of boys who went out under the auspices of the Children's Aid Society. His adventures out West will make the subject of another volume.

On the day succeeding his departure Paul was at his stand, when his attention was drawn to a man of respectable appearance, but poorly clad, and thin and emaciated, who, after a little hesitation, accosted a gentleman who was passing, in these words: "Sir, I hope you will excuse my liberty in addressing you, but I have been sick, and am without money. Can you spare me a trifle?"

"I never give to street beggars," said the gentleman, coldly.

The applicant shrank back abashed, and a look of pain and mortification overspread his features. Paul noticed it, and his heart was filled with compassion. He saw that the man was not a common street beggar; that, except under the pressure of necessity, he would not have asked help. Stepping up to him as he was slowly moving away, Paul said, gently: "Can I assist you in any way, sir?"

The other turned at the words.

"I am in great need of help," he said. "I am without money, and I have a little daughter at home who wants bread."

As he said this he came near breaking down.

"Let me help you," said Paul; and he drew a dollar from his pocket and passed it to the applicant.

"A thousand thanks for your generous kindness!" said the stranger, gratefully; "but"—and here he glanced at Paul's humble place of business—"can you spare this money?"

"Easily," said Paul. "I am doing very well, and saving up money every week."

"Then I will accept it. There are some kind hearts in the world. I felt very much depressed by the refusal I just received. It was a great sacrifice of pride for me to ask help of any one, but the thought of my little daughter removed all my scruples. I could bear privation and hunger myself, but I could not bear to see her suffer."

"Where do you live?" asked Paul.

"On Centre Street. It is a miserable place, but all I can afford."

"May I ask your business?"

"I am an artist. I came from England, my native country, some months ago, hoping to better my fortune here. But I fell sick in a short time, and continued so until a week ago."

"You are not looking well."

"I have overcome my disease, but I need nourishing food, and I have not been able to buy it."

"How did you pay your expenses while you were sick?"

"I brought over with me a small sum of money, and by great economy I made it last till a week ago. I am unknown, and, though I have two pictures finished, I cannot sell them. I was told that America was a good country for the poor; but I do not find it so for me."

"It may be, after you are known."

"But what shall I do in the meantime?"

Here an idea came to Paul. He had long intended to obtain a teacher of drawing for Jimmy. It would be a charity to employ this poor artist if he were competent.

"Did you ever give lessons in drawing?" he asked.

"Yes; I gave lessons in England. I would gladly find scholars here, but I am not known."

"I have a little brother who has a great taste for drawing," said Paul. "You may begin with him."

"Thank you," said the stranger, warmly. "You give me new hope. I will teach him gladly, and leave the price of the lessons to you."

"If you will tell me where you live I will call there at noon. You will want to buy some food for your little girl."

"Yes, poor little Mary, I must not leave her waiting any longer. I shall be very glad to see you at my poor room. It is No. — Centre Street, back room, third floor. Ask for Mr. Henderson."

"I will be sure to call."

The artist made his way to a baker's where he bought a loaf of bread. Also at a shop nearby he obtained a pint of milk, and, provided with these, he hastened home to his hungry child.

At noon, after taking lunch, Paul found his way to the address given him by the artist. The room was dark and scantily furnished. Mr. Henderson sat before an easel, trying to work. He got up hastily as Paul entered.

"I am glad to see you, my good young friend," he said. "Take a seat."

"Is this your little daughter?" asked Paul.

"Come here, Mary, and speak to the gentleman," said her father. Mary Henderson was a delicate looking little girl of eight years, with dark hair and eyes. She would have been pretty if she had been stronger and more healthy. A few weeks of good food and country air would bring back the roses to her cheeks, and fill out her emaciated form.

"Have you any pictures finished?" asked Paul.

"I have two small ones. Would you like to see them?"

"Very much."

The artist went to a closet, and produced two small pictures unframed. One was an English country landscape, pretty in design, and executed, as Paul thought, with taste.

A painting of an English country landscape.

"I like that," he said.

"The other is better," said Mr. Henderson.

He exhibited the other canvas. It was a simple sketch of a brother and sister on their way to school. The faces were bright and pretty, the attitudes natural and graceful, and all the details were well carried out.

"You are right," said Paul. "This is the best picture. The girl's face looks familiar. It is your own little girl, is it not?"

"Then you see the resemblance?"

"Yes, it is very like, but——"

"But it represents a blooming, healthful child, while my poor Mary is thin and pale. Yet when the picture was painted, before I left England, it was an exact likeness. You see what privation and the bad air of the city have done for her."

"She will look like it again. A few weeks will bring her back."

"I hope so."

"You ought to get a good price for these pictures, Mr. Henderson."

"If I had a name, I could."

"If you are willing to trust me with them, I will see what I can do for you."

"Thank you a thousand times."

"I may not be able to sell them, but I will try. Have you set a price on them?"

"No; I will sell them for anything they will fetch—for five dollars even, if no more can be obtained."

"I hope to get more."

"Mary, wrap up the pictures for the gentleman," said her father.

The little girl did so.

"If you can call on me this evening at half-past seven, Mr. Henderson," said Paul, "I will make arrangements about your giving lessons to my little brother."

"I will certainly do so."

"You will not be afraid to leave your little girl alone?"

"She can stay with a neighbor."

"Then I will expect you."

Paul wrote down his address, and took his leave, with the pictures under his arm.

He had thought of a customer. He knew that Mr. Preston was not only rich, but kindhearted and charitable. Even if he did not want the pictures, he thought he would be willing to give a small sum for them; and even a little would be of great service to the poverty-stricken artist.

He therefore made his way to Mr. Preston's counting-room, and was admitted to his presence.

"Are you busy, Mr. Preston?" asked our hero.

"Not particularly. I can spare you a few minutes."

He looked inquiringly at the parcel Paul carried under his arm.

"I have come to sell you some pictures, Mr. Preston."

"You haven't turned artist?" said the merchant, surprised.

"No; but I am acting as agent for a poor artist, who is in great need of money."

"A poor artist in both senses of the word, eh, Paul?"

"No, I think not. I am not a judge of pictures, but these seem to me very good."

"Let me see them."

Paul unrolled the bundle and displayed them. Mr. Preston took them in his hands, and examined them with interest.

"They are good pictures," he said, after a pause. "Who is the artist?"

"An Englishman named Henderson. I will tell you all I know of his story. He has been very unfortunate, and is now in pressing need of assistance."

Mr. Preston listened to the story with which the reader is already familiar. When it was concluded he said, "We must help him."

"I am going to take him as teacher for my little brother Jimmy."

"I will purchase the picture of the children for fifty dollars."

"It will be a fortune to the poor man," said Paul, joyfully.

"When shall you see him?"

"Tonight."

"Then I will give you the money to hand to him. Besides, I will give him a note to Goupil, who will allow him to exhibit the other picture in his store. That may secure its sale."

"Thank you, Mr. Preston. You will do him a great kindness."

Paul left the picture of which he had disposed, and, taking the other under his arm, went back to the necktie stand. He felt an honest pleasure in the thought of the happiness he was about to confer upon the poor artist. "It will set him on his feet," he thought.

CHAPTER XXV

MR. TALBOT'S RETURN

"Jimmy," said Paul, on reaching home, "there is a gentleman coming to see you this evening."

"A gentleman—to see me?" repeated the little boy, in surprise.

"Yes. Mr. Henderson."

"But I don't know him."

"You will know him very soon. He is an artist, and is going to give you lessons."

"How good you are, Paul!" said Jimmy, joyfully; "but," he added, considerately, "won't you have to pay him a good deal?"

"No; he is a poor man, and it is partly to help him that I have engaged him to give you lessons. I expect him in an hour. So get out your best drawings, so that he will see how far you are advanced."

"Does he paint pictures? I should like to see some of them."

"I have one with me."

"Oh, let me see it!"

Paul removed the paper from the painting he had brought with him, and displayed it to his little brother.

"It is beautiful, Paul. I wonder if I can ever paint such a nice picture."

"No doubt you can, if you study faithfully. I brought away another of Mr. Henderson's pictures, which I like better than this, but I have sold it to Mr. Preston."

"How much did you get for it?"

"Fifty dollars."

"Isn't that a large price?" asked Mrs. Hoffman.

"Not for a good picture. I dare say Jimmy will by and by be charging as much as that for a picture."

"I hope so, Paul. I would like to earn some money."

"You are too young to earn money now, Jimmy. That will come in good time."

Soon after the dinner table was cleared Mr. Henderson called.

"I am glad to see you, Mr. Henderson," said Paul, cordially. "This is my mother, Mrs. Hoffman, and here is the young scholar I told you of."

Jimmy looked up shyly.

"He has seen your picture and likes it. By the way, I have sold one of your pictures—the one introducing the children."

"Thank you for your kindness," said the artist, his face brightening. "You have done what I could not do, and it will give me very welcome aid."

"I hope the price will be satisfactory," said Paul.

"I did not expect much," said Mr. Henderson, who inferred that the price obtained was small. "I am unknown, and I have no right to expect much for my work."

"I sold it to a friend of mine for fifty dollars," continued Paul.

"Fifty dollars!" exclaimed the poor artist, hardly crediting the testimony of his ears.

"Yes," said Paul, enjoying his surprise. "Is it satisfactory?"

"Satisfactory! It is ten times as much as I expected. How can I ever thank you?" said Mr. Henderson, seizing Paul's hand in his fervent gratitude.

"The purchaser is rich, and he has promised to speak a word to Goupil in your favor."

"Heaven sent you to my help," said the artist. "What a change has a single day wrought! This morning I woke without a penny, and my poor child without bread. Tonight I am rich, and Hope has once more visited me. I owe all my good fortune to you. Will you permit me to give lessons to your brother without charge?"

"No," said Paul, decidedly. "I think every one ought to be paid for their work. What I have done for you has given me very little trouble. I am glad that I could help you. I know what it is to be poor, and most people would call me poor now; but I can earn enough for our expenses, and lay up something besides, so I do not feel poor. Now, Jimmy, go and bring your drawings, and show the gentleman."

The drawings were brought, and, to Jimmy's delight, elicited warm approval from the artist.

"Your brother has great talent," said he. "I shall be very glad to have him for a pupil. It is much pleasanter to teach where the scholar has taste and talent. When would you like the lessons to begin?"

"As soon as possible. Tomorrow, if you can come."

"And at what time?"

"At any time. I suppose the day would be better."

"Yes, it would be better, on account of the light. Besides, I like to be with my little daughter in the evening."

"Have you a little daughter?" asked Mrs. Hoffman.

"Yes, madam. She must be nearly the age of my young pupil here."

"Bring her with you at any time," said motherly Mrs. Hoffman. "I shall be glad to have her come."

"If she would not be in the way."

"Not at all. We have plenty of room, and Jimmy has no playmate. We shall be very glad to see her."

"Mary will enjoy coming," said her father. "I appreciate your kindness in inviting her."

"By the way, Mr. Henderson," suggested Paul, "why don't you move into the upper part of the city? It will be more convenient for you, especially if you get other pupils."

"It is a good plan," said the artist. "I could not do so before, because I had no money. Now, thanks to your kindness, I can do so."

It was arranged that Jimmy should take two lessons a week, for which Paul agreed to pay a dollar each. The sum was small, but to Mr. Henderson it was an important help. I will anticipate the future so far as to say that, after a while, through the persistent efforts of Paul, aided by Mr. Preston, he obtained three other pupils, from whom he was able to obtain a higher price, and occasionally he effected the sale of a picture, so that he was able to occupy more comfortable rooms, and provide himself with better clothing. The days of his adversity were over, and he now enjoyed a moderate degree of prosperity. Little Mary regained her lost flesh and color, and once more looked as she did when she sat for the figure of the girl in her father's picture, which Paul had sold to Mr. Preston. She came often with her father, when he was to give a lesson to Jimmy, and sometimes Mrs. Hoffman called to invite her to accompany Jimmy and herself to Central Park.

As to Jimmy, he surprised his teacher by the rapid progress which he made. He would have devoted all his time to drawing if his mother had permitted, but she was not willing that he should neglect his school studies—for Jimmy now attended school. His health, too, had improved, and he no longer looked weak and delicate.

So several months passed away. Paul's business continued good. It did not increase much, for there was not an opportunity for that. But he averaged fifteen dollars a week profit, and that, he justly felt, was a very good income from such a limited business. Mrs. Hoffman continued to make ties for Paul, so she, too, earned three or four dollars a week, and as they had no house rent to pay, they were able not only to live very comfortably, paying all the bills promptly, but to save up money besides. In addition to the money in Mr. Preston's hands, Paul had an account at a downtown savings-bank, which already amounted to over two hundred dollars.

"We must save money now, mother," said Paul; "for Mr. Talbot will be coming home by and by, and then we shall have to look up other rooms, and pay rent."

"Do you know when he means to come home? Has Mr. Preston told you?"

"No, mother. I think I will call round in the morning and inquire. He has already been away more than a year."

When Paul entered Mr. Preston's counting-room the next morning that gentleman looked up from his desk, and said, "I was just about to write you a letter, Paul."

"Indeed, sir."

"Yes; I am in receipt of a letter from Mr. Talbot, in which he announces his immediate return home. He will be here in four weeks, and he desires your mother to engage women to clean the house thoroughly, and put it in order for his occupation. Of course, you will keep an account of all you have to expend in this way, and you can hand me the bill."

"Yes, sir. I will see that it is done."

Paul heard, with some regret, of Mr. Talbot's speedy return. It would curtail his income considerably. Still he felt that Mr. Talbot would be satisfied with the manner in which his mother and himself had acquitted themselves of their trust, and that was a source of satisfaction.

He gave his mother immediate notice of the approaching return of Mr. Talbot, and she began to look about for rooms to which to remove. At length she found a very comfortable place at twenty dollars a month. Half that sum would have obtained them shelter in a poor tenement house, but both Paul and his mother had become fastidious, and felt that such economy would be out of place. They must have a respectable and comfortable home, even if they were prevented thereby from adding so much to their account at the savings-bank.

At length the steamer in which the Talbots had taken passage arrived. A coach brought them from the pier to the house. Mrs. Hoffman and Paul were in waiting to receive them. Mrs. Talbot expressed herself pleased with the neat appearance of the house, and Mr. Talbot called Paul aside.

"My young friend," he said, "I deferred, till my return home, the acknowledgment of your very creditable conduct in the defense of my house. You showed a coolness and good judgment remarkable in one of your age. In return for this, and in acknowledgment of the generally satisfactory manner in which you and your mother have kept my house, I ask your acceptance of this wallet, with its contents."

When Paul opened it he was astonished and delighted to find that it contained two one-hundred dollar bills.

"One of them properly belongs to you, mother," he said. But Mrs. Hoffman refused to take it.

"No, Paul," she said, "you are the treasurer of our little household. Take this money and add to your savings. Some time you will find it useful in enlarging your business, or entering upon a new one."

"I will put it in the savings-bank, as you recommend, mother; but you must remember that the fund there is yours as much as mine."

"I will promise to call for money, Paul, whenever I want it. I like to think that we have so large a fund to draw upon in case of need.

CHAPTER XXVI

FROM THE SIDEWALK TO THE SHOP

One morning, some months later, Paul was looking over the advertising columns of the Herald. As his eye glanced carelessly over the Chances for Business, his attention was drawn to the following:

"FOR SALE The stock and fixtures of a gentlemen's small furnishing store. Good reasons for selling. Apply at No. — Sixth Avenue."

"I wonder how much it would cost," thought Paul. "I wish I had a small store instead of a stand. I could make more money. Besides, it would be more comfortable in cold and stormy weather."

It was a raw morning in November. Paul had his hands in his pockets, and had much ado to keep warm. But he knew that worse days were to come. The winter before he had suffered not a little on some days when he felt the necessity of keeping at his business.

"Let me see," he reflected. "I have about six hundred dollars. That is something, but it wouldn't go far toward stocking a store. Still, I have a great mind to go up and look at the place, and inquire about terms."

The more Paul thought about it, the more he felt a desire to go. He accordingly got a boy, in whom he felt confidence, to attend his stand, while he himself jumped on a Sixth Avenue car and rode up to the shop advertised.

On entering he found it small, but neat, and to all appearance a good stand for business. The proprietor, a man of thirty-five or thereabouts, came forward.

"What can I show you?" he asked.

"I saw your advertisement in the Herald," said Paul, "and came to inquire about it. You want to sell out?"

"Yes. It is on account of my wife's health. The doctor says the city air doesn't agree with her, and orders her into the country. I don't want to be separated from her, and, besides, I have a chance to open a store in a country town where my uncle lives."

"Is this a good stand for business?"

"Excellent. I am making more money here than I can expect to outside of the city; but of course that is not to be put in the scale

---

against my wife's health. Were you thinking of going into the business?"

"I should like to, but I have not much capital. At what price do you value your stock?"

"At two thousand dollars."

"That is more money than I have got."

"I'll tell you what I will do. If you will give me a thousand dollars down, and give me good security for the balance, payable a year hence, I will sell out to you."

"What is the rent?"

"A thousand dollars."

"Isn't that a good deal?"

"In proportion to the value of my stock, it is, but I keep turning it over. Last year, after paying rent and all expenses, including wages to a boy of seventeen, who assisted me, I cleared two thousand dollars."

To Paul this seemed considerable. It would be a great improvement upon his present position, and he would enjoy much more being the owner of a store than of a street stand. But where would he get the money?

"Couldn't you take less than a thousand dollars down?" he asked.

The man shook his head.

"I need that amount at once," he said. "You had better accept my terms. You can't do better. Can't you raise the money somewhere?"

"I will see," said Paul.

He had thought of Mr. Preston. He knew that Mr. Preston was his friend, and that he was fully able to assist him. He would go and see him, and consult him about the matter, not directly asking him for help, but giving him an opportunity to offer.

"I will come back tomorrow and give you my answer," he said.

"Come tonight, if you can."

"Very well, I will, if possible."

Paul was fortunate enough to find Mr. Preston in.

"Good-morning, Paul," said the merchant, pleasantly; "what can I do for you this morning?"

"I want to consult you on a matter of business, Mr. Preston."

"I shall be glad to advise you as well as I can."

Hereupon Paul explained the matter, first displaying the advertisement.

"Do you think the shop favorably situated for business?" asked Mr. Preston.

"Yes, sir."

"Is it pretty well stocked?"

"Yes, sir. If I had it I might want to increase the stock a little."

"So the man asks a thousand dollars cash?"

"Yes, sir."

"How much money have you?"

"Six hundred."

"Well, Paul, I think favorably of your plan. If you want to take the shop, I will lend you the money you need, and stand security for the remainder."

"Thank you, sir," said Paul, joyfully.

"Wait a minute till you hear my conditions. This is strictly a business arrangement between us. I expect you to pay me interest at the legal rate, and to pay it punctually as it falls due. You understand that?"

"Yes, sir, that is only fair."

"As you say, it is only fair, yet borrowers are apt to forget it. They will make all sorts of promises when they want to borrow, and break them afterward. Even honest men will think it is enough to pay interest whenever it is convenient, forgetting that by their neglect they are injuring their credit. Some years since I helped two former clerks to establish themselves in business. Both were honest; but while one was prompt in all his engagements, and waited upon me on the very day the interest came due with the money ready, the other obliged me to send for it, and then put me off on every occasion, though he paid finally. The result was, that after a while I assisted the first cheerfully to extend his business. The second, hearing of it, made a similar application, which I promptly refused. Do you wonder at it?"

"Not at all, sir. I think you were perfectly right."

"Be prompt in all your engagements. That is a good rule in business, and in everything else. I have confidence in your integrity, and shall be very glad to assist you. Go and finish your negotiation, and when you want the money come to me."

"Thank you, sir, not only for your kind offer, but for your advice."

"He is going to succeed," said the merchant, as Paul went out. "He will some day be a prosperous man."

The merchant was pleased at the respect with which his advice was received. Young America is very apt to regard the counsel of the old and experienced as of slight value; but in this they make a great mistake. There are plenty of young men, who, from their own self-sufficiency and impatience of good advice, go to financial ruin every year. He shows wisdom who avails himself of the experience of other men, avoiding their errors, and imitating what in them is worthy of imitation.

Paul returned to the shop and made a careful examination of the stock. He came to the conclusion that the price asked was not excessive, and agreed to pay it. In the course of two days the transfer was concluded, and Paul transferred the small stock of his necktie stand to the shop which he had taken. During all this time he had said nothing to his mother of the change he had made. He wanted to surprise her.

"Mother," he said, on the second morning of his possession, "I want you to take a little walk with me this morning."

"May I go too, Paul?" asked Jimmy.

"Yes, Jimmy, I meant to invite you. So get your cap."

"Where shall we walk to, Paul?" asked his mother.

"I don't mean to tell you just yet. You will soon know."

"Is it a secret?" asked Mrs. Hoffman, smiling.

"Yes; it is a great secret."

"Then I will try to stifle my curiosity for a time."

"What is it, Paul? Whisper it to me," said Jimmy.

"You must wait, too," said Paul. "I believe you are more curious than mother."

They had not far to walk. When they reached the shop the sign told them nothing, for Paul had not yet had time to have his own put up. He had given the order to a sign-painter, but it would take time to fulfill it.

"I want to go in here a minute," he said.

"Shall we wait outside?" asked his mother.

"No; come in. I would like to have you see the shop."

The three entered. A young clerk, who had been in the employ of the former proprietor, and whom Paul had agreed to retain at the same wages, was behind the counter.

"Good-morning, Mr. Hoffman," he said.

"Have you sold anything this morning?" asked Paul.

"Yes, sir; I have entered the sales on the slate."

"Let me see them."

"A new style of necktie is out. I think it will be well to get it. It was asked for this morning."

"Very well. Just make a memorandum of it."

"Paul," said Mrs. Hoffman, who had listened to the conversation in surprise, "have you anything to do with this store?"

"I am the proprietor," answered Paul, smiling.

"Is it true? How did it happen?"

"I wanted to surprise you, mother, and so I told you nothing about it."

"When did you come into it?"

"This is only the second day. Mr. Preston helped me, or I could not have carried out the arrangement."

"Do you think you can pay all your expenses and make money?" asked Mrs. Hoffman, a little frightened when she heard of the rent which Paul had agreed to pay.

"I mean to try, mother. I don't feel much afraid. I shall devote myself faithfully to business, and if I don't do well it won't be my fault."

We have kept our promise, and shown how Paul advanced slowly but surely from the humble position of a street merchant to be the proprietor of a shop. Now that several years have elapsed, I am able to say that he succeeded, even beyond his anticipations. At the end of two years he took a larger shop and engaged two extra clerks. Prompt in his engagements, and of thorough integrity, he is likely to be even more prosperous as the years roll on.

A men's clothing store like the one Paul ends up owning.

His mother is no longer dependent upon him. Mr. Henderson, the English artist, now able to obtain purchasers for his pictures at remunerative prices, asked her to become his wife and a mother to his little girl, and, after a little hesitation, she consented, partly, I think, because Jimmy liked the artist so much. Mr. Henderson took pains to instruct Jimmy and develop his talent, with such encouraging success that Paul's prediction seems likely to be fulfilled, and I shall not be surprised if the name of James Hoffman should, before many years, rank among the most prominent in the list of our artists.

Julius, as I have already stated, left the streets of New York for a home in the West. His old enemies, Jack Morgan and Tom Marlowe, were sentenced to a long imprisonment in Sing Sing. Marlowe threatens vengeance upon Julius whenever he gets free from prison. Whether he will have an opportunity of carrying out his threat I cannot tell.

THE END

~ ~ ~

TEACHERS GUIDE QUESTIONS FOR SLOW AND SURE

1. We catch up with Paul Hoffman six months after Paul the Peddler. How has his situation improved? What has made this possible?

2. What happens that makes Paul and his family seek new housing? Why are they not upset about having to do so?

3. Paul considers the offer to live in the Talbot house as a way to get rich by saving $20 every month. How are they saving $20 a month when they were only paying $6 in their old place?

4. Paul looks to the future and says that he'll one day live in a house as nice as the Talbot house. What gives him this hope? What is the author trying to say here?

5. What makes Mr. and Mrs. Talbot decide to entrust the Hoffman family with their house?

6. At one point in this story, Paul's mother is concerned that he is spending his money unwisely. Is his money well spent? Why or why not?

7. What makes Paul help Julius? What does this tell you about Paul's character?

8. Describe Julius' living situation. What impact has it had on his beliefs?

9. Julius helps a man at the free lunch saloon. How did he do it? What message is the author sending here?

10. What makes Julius turn on his companions? How does he do this?

11. Two different opinions are given in this book about what makes people successful. What are they?

12. What regret does Jimmy Hoffman make Julius feel? Why does he feel this regret?

13. How have Paul's good deeds come to reward him? What is the author trying to teach with Paul's whole story?

TEACHERS GUIDE ANSWERS FOR SLOW AND SURE

1.   Paul's situation has improved greatly since Paul the Peddler. In the six months since the first book, he has been able to save up more than $100. Along with the $150 gaining interest with Mr. Preston, their financial security has gotten a lot better.

2.   A man falling asleep with a cigarette burned down their apartment building. Since they were so poor, they didn't lose a lot of possessions. It also pushes them into finding better living accommodations, since they can now afford it.

3.   They're saving $20 instead of $6 every month because they had already budgeted $20 to spend on rent every month. They no longer have to do this. It's an economic concept called "opportunity cost."

4.   Paul believes that he will one day live in a house as nice as the Talbot house because he has seen plenty of young boys work their way up from the streets, and has faith that he can do the same himself.

5.   Mr. Talbot entrusts the Hoffman family on Mr. Preston's recommendation alone. Mrs. Talbot is pleased by the appearance and personality of Paul's mother, and thinks she would be the right person to look after their house.

6.   Paul's money is well spent, because he manages to spend it in ways that bring him rewards. New clothes for himself and Jimmy make them look more presentable to Mrs. Talbot.

7.   Paul helps Julius because he knew what it was like to be as hungry as Julius was. This shows that Paul is a very compassionate person who doesn't want to see good people suffer.

8.   Julius lives with two career criminals in Jack and Marlowe. While it hasn't provided the most stable living situation, it has managed to give him a sense of what he doesn't want to become.

9.   Julius gives the man at the free lunch saloon money to buy a drink, therefore entitling him to lunch. The author makes sure to talk about how good it feels to help someone in need.

10. Julius makes the final decision to turn on his companions when he hears Jack talk of abandoning him to move to California. He also sees the struggles of the two criminals, and doesn't want to end up like them.

11. Paul's opinion is that hard work and honesty make someone successful. Jack and Marlowe believe that people are only successful because they have money.

12. Jimmy Hoffman makes Julius regret his lack of an education. He feels this regret because he believes that nobody can be successful without an education.

13. Through good deeds, Paul manages to advance himself from a street peddler to a street merchant, and then eventually to a store owner. His good deeds also save his family from burglars, secure an art education for his brother and even find a husband for his widow mother. The author is saying that good deeds and hard work will be rewarded.

THE LIFE AND THEMES OF

HORATIO ALGER, JR.

By Stefan Kanfer

The Merriam-Webster Dictionary devotes one sentence to him: "Of, relating to, or resembling the fiction of Horatio Alger in which success is achieved through self-reliance and hard work."

True as far as it goes, but that sentence reveals nothing about the man or his accomplishment. Then again, other contemporary reference books are just as terse. Not one acknowledges that Alger in his day (circa 1880-1920) was a publishing phenomenon. During those decades, when a sale of 10,000 volumes was deemed a triumph, readers bought more than 200 million copies of Alger's works, placing him in a league with J.K. Rowling and Stephen King.

Alas, today most of his novels—and there are more than 100—are out of print. But not for long. Thanks to the resuscitation efforts of Sumner Books, a division of Creators Syndicate, Alger's best literary productions are being furnished with fresh covers, new fonts and energetic promotion.

Seldom has there been a more relevant illustration of the maxim that what goes around comes around. At the turn of the 19th century, Alger was the standard-bearer of a phenomenally successful experiment in social reform and personal improvement. That movement inspired disadvantaged kids to move on up, leading juvenile delinquents into productive, significant lives. Men as different as Groucho Marx and Ernest Hemingway were fans.

"Horatio Alger's books conveyed a powerful message to me," wrote Marx, "and to many of my young friends as well—that if you worked hard at your trade, the big chance would eventually come. As a child I didn't regard it as a myth, and as an old man I think of it as the story of my life."

Hemingway's sister Marcelline recalled that during their childhood, "There was one summer when Ernest couldn't get enough of Horatio Alger." Not that Alger's boys' books influenced Papa's prose style. But there must have been something in the writer's stress on grit and self-reliance that affected young Ernest, as it did so many of his contemporaries.

By the end of the Roaring Twenties, though, Horatio Alger had become as passé as the Ford Model T. During the Depression he fared no better; Nathaniel West's satirical 1934 novel, A Cool Million, sent Alger's plots in reverse, as the naïve protagonist loses limb after limb seeking success among rapacious capitalists. Decades later, the film adaptation of Hunter Thompson's 1971 novel, Fear and Loathing in Las Vegas, presented the antihero as "Horatio Alger gone mad on drugs in Las Vegas."

What lay behind Alger's ability to enchant so many Americans—and to enrage so many others? The author's story furnishes a trove of clues:

The sickly child of a Unitarian minister in Marlborough, Massachusetts, Horatio, born in 1832, was always the smallest in his class and far from an academic star. Still, his report cards were good enough for admission to Harvard. There his academic prowess was in inverse proportion to his size (5 feet 2 inches). He won prizes, published verse and fiction in undergraduate magazines, and labeled the entire four years a period of "unmixed happiness."

Decades would pass before he found such contentment again. Upon graduation, Horatio attempted to make his way as a writer. After five unsuccessful years, he returned to Harvard, this time to study at the Divinity School. In 1860 the Reverend Horatio Alger was named minister of the First Parish Unitarian Church of Brewster on Cape Cod. Salary: $800 per year. To supplement his meager income, he turned once again to writing. This time, his stories were well-received, and he allowed himself to dream of a dual career of preacher and writer. That's when catastrophe struck.

It was of his own making, if one historian is to be believed. According to this claim, a 13-year-old told his parents that the new parson had made advances to him. An investigation began. Another lad made a similar complaint. Faced with charges of behaving inappropriately, the accused was allowed to resign—with the proviso that he leave town at once.

Sometime later, Horatio wrote a poem about one Friar Anselmo, who had committed an unspecified crime. Melancholy and remorseful, he comes across a wounded traveler and gives him aid. Whereupon an angel materializes and offers salvation:

Thy guilty stains shall be washed white again
By noble service done thy fellow man.

The fugitive repaired to New York City in the spring of 1866, resolved to live out the Christian ideal, expiating his sin by saving others. The Manhattan he entered was the epicenter of the Gilded Age, a magnet for millions of ambitious climbers, drawn by the post-Civil War boom. Out of sight of the glittering prosperity, the mansions and carriages, however, was another New York, a squalid night town that travelers compared to Calcutta, India.

In The Good Old Days, They Were Terrible, historian Otto Bettmann reports that there was scarcely a slum that pedestrians could negotiate "without climbing over a heap of trash or, in rain, wading through a bed of slime." Many streets were so dangerous that policemen hesitated to walk them alone. A Gramercy Park resident noted in his diary, "Most of my friends are investing in revolvers and carry them about at night"—and the Park was one of the city's better neighborhoods.

The New York City street urchin entered the national consciousness in those years. More than 60,000 neglected or abandoned kids ran unsupervised in the street, partly because of the fallout from the tidal waves of immigration from Europe and partly because of families broken by the Civil War.

What was to be done about these juveniles likely to die on the streets or to end up behind bars? The Reverend Charles Loring Brace founded the Children's Aid Society, designed to take homeless or abused kids away from their corrosive environments. At the same time, John Hughes, New York's first Roman Catholic archbishop, set up parochial schools and a residential institution called the Catholic Protectory, which brought up abandoned or orphaned children to be useful members of society.

Horatio Alger joined these efforts at reclamation. He, too, asked himself what could be done about homeless children. Seeking answers, he wandered through the city's worst neighborhoods. He interviewed "street arabs" who spoke of broken homes, violent confrontations with parents, doomed futures. He observed how their cocky attitudes masked a profound despair. He advised them to get real jobs instead of hanging about, squandering whatever came their way from shining shoes or picking pockets. A handful nodded in agreement, expressing the desire to change their lives; most were content to take life as they found it.

Why, he pondered, did individuals subjected to the same conditions turn out so differently? One boy might become a thief, a sociopath, even a killer. His neighbor, perhaps his brother, might aim to be an upright citizen. What was the difference between them?

What saved certain boys, he came to believe, was a quality that gave them the strength to resist sloth and temptation. In a word, character. But was this inborn? In that case determinism won the day, and change was out of the question. Or, given the right opportunity and attitude, could a dispossessed youth win his share of the American dream? The latter, Alger believed—but only if the boy stopped regarding himself as a victim.

As Alger meditated upon the worst crime of the slums—the stealing of childhood from children—an idea came to him. He would be Brother Anselmo redivivus. He had sinned against youths; now he would rescue them—and in the process save himself. As the novelist put it, by depicting the situation of city waifs, he would "excite a deeper and more widespread sympathy in the public mind, as well as exert a salutary influence upon the class of whom he is writing, by setting before them inspiring examples of what energy, ambition, and an honest purpose may achieve."

Ragged Dick became the template of the fiction to follow. Subtitled Street Life in New York with the Boot Blacks, it charted the rise of a 14-year-old boy from poverty to prosperity. Dick Hunter is an adolescent with all odds against him. He has no family, he smokes, drinks alcohol when he can afford it—not very often on the small change he gets from shining gentlemen's shoes—and sleeps on gratings in the winter.

Yet something separates him from his fellow waifs. He refuses to pick pockets like the others, won't mock his elders, and yearns to "grow up 'spectable.'" His bearing and his innate decency attract the attention of upright New Yorkers. One introduces him to his church; another presents Dick with a few dollars.

The earnest youth resolves to become literate to save his money and live a clean life. One day on a walk near South Ferry he sees a toddler fall in the water. Without hesitation, Dick jumps in and saves the drowning child. In gratitude, the father, an affluent businessman, offers the rescuer a job in his office. Gainfully employed, the onetime vagabond Dick Hunter becomes Richard Hunter Esq., and shuts the door forever on the "old vagabond life which he hoped never to resume."

Naïve? Simplistic? To the jaded, the cynical and the ignorant, yes. But not to thousands of children trapped in the real world of poverty and early death. They got the message of Ragged Dick and demanded more Horatio Alger novels with more moral lessons for them to absorb. Those books changed—and in many cases saved—lives a century before Dr. Martin Luther King Jr. stated his belief that what mattered was not the color of one's skin but the content of one's character.

Today, if you listen closely you can hear, amid the jeers, the escalating sound of the last laugh. In 1947, the Horatio Alger Association was founded. It attracts more prominent men and women now than it did then. The group is dedicated to recognizing American leaders who rose, like Alger's young heroes, from humble origins "through honesty, hard work, self-reliance and perseverance." With grants to U.S. high-school students who have "faced and overcome great obstacles in their young lives," the association encourages them to emulate such enterprising and disparate members as Oprah Winfrey and Ray Kroc, Tom Brokaw and Maya Angelou, Stan Musial and Colin Powell.

They can all testify to the truths that lie between the covers of this volume. Turn the first few pages, and you'll understand why so many followed Horatio Alger's breathless, cliff-hanging chapters leading the way from skid row to success. And why so many more are about to read that map in a world where everything has changed—except the basic truths of life.

Stefan Kanfer is an award-winning writer for City Journal and the author of numerous best-selling books.

ABOUT HORATIO ALGER, JR.

Horatio Alger was born in 1832 in Chelsea, Massachusetts. He spent his early years in the small town and under the guidance of the church and his father, the town pastor, before the family moved just west of Boston to the town of Marlborough.

As a shy young boy, Alger poured himself into books and soon became a distinguished student. He studied at Harvard and Harvard Divinity School before becoming a minister. He practiced ministry for a few years near Boston and on Cape Cod, but he was distracted by his true passion: writing.

He loved to write, and by 1865 Alger had written a handful of stories, including Frank's Campaign and Paul Prescott's Charge. The latter was the first in a series of stories that would eventually lead to his great success. In 1866, Alger moved to New York to write poetry, newspaper stories and magazine articles. However, he was shocked to find so many homeless and forgotten children among the streets, an unfortunate consequence of the Civil War. He made it his duty to aid the condition of these lost children, both through his stories and by his continuous acts of benevolence.

Horatio Alger became a household name shortly after the Civil War when he began publishing stories in the form of serializations. These serializations were featured in magazines such as Student and Schoolmate and were later compiled as books. Alger's books became enormously popular, especially among teenage boys across the country, and they soon reached millions and millions of readers. Alger continued to produce several stories a year, and, in later years, wrote novels in and of themselves instead of novels from magazine serials.

The years immediately following the Civil War were the same years when the United States emerged as one nation on the road to becoming a worldwide empire. The years between 1865 and 1900 were the years of the empire builders, with the rags-to-riches stories of John D. Rockefeller, Andrew Carnegie, Cornelius Vanderbilt and Thomas Edison. They were the years that laid the foundation for Henry Ford and other business titans and for the spectacular growth of the American economy throughout the 20th century and through today. During these years, Alger published well over 100 stories, poems and novels that spoke to the timeless themes and successes of this era.

The theme of Alger's books is consistent: If you work hard, go the extra mile, are faithful and honest, show kindness and generosity, and maintain a cheerful, positive and optimistic attitude, you will succeed in creating financial security and happiness. On the other hand, if you lie, cheat, steal, are lazy or envious, and try to take advantage of other people, you will be doomed to failure and misery. Despite his background as a preacher, Alger does not make these points in a self-righteous or pontificating way. What he does instead -- just like the parables that Jesus told -- is to create stories that illustrate the virtues that lead to success. And the stories that Alger creates are no ordinary stories. Each one is filled with lively plots and twists and turns, ones that are always unexpected and keep the reader wanting to know what's going to happen next.

As Alger grew older, he continuously strived to write the Great American Novel, little realizing that the rags-to-riches stories he created were more influential than any other novelists'. He travelled out west in early 1877 searching for new material and returned near the end of the year, producing similar stories with a new western backdrop. By 1897, Alger was suffering from asthma, bronchitis and slight short-term memory loss. He moved in with his sister in South Natick, Massachusetts where he spent the last two years of his life.

Most people have never heard of Horatio Alger while some are vaguely familiar with the term "rags-to-riches." In the Alger family, it was the norm to burn correspondence and manuscripts, and this, coupled with Alger's shyness, has greatly kept him from history's limelight. Though too often forgotten today, Alger's works and the themes within them still affect the American psyche. Many assert that there is a lagging spirit in present American culture, that these inspiring stories are irrelevant. Young people are bombarded with external stimuli that make it difficult for them to get to know themselves. Wide-eyed innocence and childlike enthusiasm, once revered as admirable qualities, are sources of mockery and disdain, which makes cynicism and pessimism inevitable. Video games, television shows, movies and music are all aimed at titillating and at seeing who can be the most gritty, violent or shocking. More than a few commentators have used the word "degrading" to describe the assault that children encounter today.

This is unfortunate. Young people need heroes and role models today just as much as they did in the 1870s and '80s, when Alger was creating them at a feverish pace from his New York City apartment, writing as many as four books at a time. Publisher A.K. Loring asserted that Alger's books "captured the spirits of reborn America" for "above all you can hear the cry of triumph of the oppressed over the oppressor … What Alger has done is to portray the soul – the ambitious soul – of the country." Years later, biographer Edwin P. Hoyt concludes that Alger is "a writer whose influence on the American scene has been so profound that it is hard to measure." Indeed, Alger's works made an overwhelming impression on American culture and society that are still alive with us today. It is for this reason that these classics must be brought to a new generation of readers.

OUR COMMITMENT TO
HORATIO ALGER

By Rick Newcombe

Sumner Books is totally committed to reviving interest in Horatio Alger, one of the best-selling authors of all time yet someone who has been all but forgotten today. I'd like to tell you how this project came about.

Probably the best starting point is to tell you a little about myself. I grew up in suburban Chicago, and my parents were religious and fundamentally optimistic in their outlook on life. They encouraged all eight of their children to be positive in our thinking and hope and pray for the best in all situations. In my adolescence, I discovered many of the self-help authors from the 20th century, including Dale Carnegie, Napoleon Hill and Norman Vincent Peale. I remember reading a small magazine in the 1970s, when I was in my 20s, called Success Unlimited and being inspired each month to work hard and stay positive. The publisher of this magazine was W. Clement Stone, who started his career selling insurance policies door to door and who went on to build Combined Insurance, which became part of Aon, one of the largest insurance companies in the world.

By the time Mr. Stone died in 2002, he was a very successful businessman, an extremely generous philanthropist and totally committed to spreading the gospel of positive thinking. I remember reading one of his books, The Success System That Never Fails, which was both an autobiography and a blueprint for achieving success. Stone told the story of spending a summer on a farm in Michigan when he was 12, getting fresh air, helping on the farm and enjoying picnics, carnivals and camping out.

W. Clement Stone

"But I'll never forget the first day I went upstairs to the attic," he wrote, "for there I met Horatio Alger. At least 50 of his books, dusty and weather-worn, were piled in the corner. I took one down to the hammock in the front yard and started to read."

Stone said he was so enthralled he couldn't stop. "I read through all of them that summer," he wrote.

He said the principle in each book was that "the hero became a success because he was a man of character -- the villain a failure because he deceived and embezzled. How many Alger books were sold? No one knows. Estimates range from 100 million to 300 million. We do know that his books inspired thousands of American boys from poor families to strive to do the right thing because it was right and to acquire wealth."

That was the first time I had heard of Horatio Alger, but it never occurred to me to try to find his books. Over the years, I founded Creators Syndicate, which became one of the most successful newspaper syndication companies in the world. I attribute much of our success to our positive thinking and upbeat attitude. We became a multimillion-dollar international corporation by syndicating a wide variety of journalists, celebrities and award-winning cartoonists.

As we were expanding into new businesses, e-books and audiobooks were a natural starting point because we work with so many talented writers and artists. But we also wanted to try new things. With that in mind, I remembered Mr. Stone's enthusiastic recommendation of Horatio Alger's books, and I decided to read some. Many were available as e-books, and I thoroughly enjoyed them.

I had a good feeling whenever I was transported back to New York City as it was in 1870, when trains were called "cars" and there were no automobiles. There was a constant risk of crossing the streets without streetlights or walk signs. A number of years later, the Brooklyn Dodgers, now the Los Angeles Dodgers, got their name from the treacherous dodging of horses, wagons and streetcars that was required to cross the street in the city. In those days, plumbing with hot and cold running water was not taken for granted, much less radios, televisions, computers or smartphones. Are you kidding? A smartphone in the 1860s? There wasn't even a telephone.

But what great stories Alger wrote -- one after another. I couldn't get enough of them! And it was impossible not to feel grateful for all the modern conveniences of the 21st century when immersing myself in the world of America as it was in the 1860s and '70s.

As I read book after book, I felt like a teenager all over again, excited about the future and the promise of a brighter tomorrow. It was then that I decided to go full bore into spreading the word of Horatio Alger.

One of the problems with the e-books was the lack of organization; another was the maddening number of typos, over and over and over, or the lack of illustrations or the lack of a table of contents. In fact, what was intended to be a good deed to spread Mr. Alger's message really turned out to be something of a disservice.

So I made it my mission to have professional editors edit the texts so there were no typographical or spelling errors. We found appropriate illustrations. We included detailed tables of contents for each book, and we decided to publish them in groups, when appropriate, which has never been done before. We are including commentaries and teachers guides with each e-book.

We also decided to make audiobooks of as many of these "Stories of Success" as possible. We hired a terrific actor, Ben Gillman, and his initial experience shows you how far we have to go to spread the word. Ben went to the Hollywood public library to find some Horatio Alger books, but there was none. "You'd have to go to the downtown public library, in the historical section, to find those," the librarian told him.

Remember, this is one of the best-selling American authors of all time, yet it is as if he never existed.

Part of the problem is that some of the caricatures of Horatio Alger over the years have been absolutely brutal. Even to this day, the Encyclopedia Britannica, from which we expect objective reporting, calls Alger's dialogue and plots "outrageously bad." Come again? The encyclopedia is supposed to provide broad knowledge on specific subjects, not offer the biased literary criticism of a handful of editors. Talk about being unfair -- and just plain wrong!

How do you answer a cheap shot like that? Really, it is nothing more than an incredibly snooty opinion; in fact, it is an "outrageously bad" opinion. Remember, the Horatio Alger books were intended to be not great literature but rather inspirational stories to motivate young boys to achieve a better life. If the dialogue and plots were not lively and believable, the books would not have sold in the millions. The fact that Horatio Alger helped form the American character shows that an incredible number of boys ate up his books as thrilling and believable.

The brilliant writer Stefan Kanfer wrote an extensive review of Horatio Alger's works in 2000 for City Journal magazine, a publication of the prestigious Manhattan Institute. He started off believing the critics, but when he actually read some of Horatio Alger's books, he drew a totally different conclusion. "I began reading the novels aloud to my children," he wrote. "We found them well-plotted, entertaining, and instructive, not at all the righteous antiquities that I had been led to believe. Almost every chapter ends with a cliff-hanger, and all of us could hardly wait for the next night to find out what happened. The conclusions never failed to produce an emotional satisfaction and a feeling that what the author was selling -- independence, forbearance, square dealing -- was well worth buying."

We can only speculate about why the critics have been so harsh on Horatio Alger, but no doubt some it stems from their being turned off by precisely the character traits that Mr. Kanfer identifies. Like it or not, there is a mindset that scoffs at individual achievement through hard work, a positive attitude and generosity -- living every day with an "attitude of gratitude," which is the essence of Horatio Alger's message.

W. Clement Stone was routinely mocked for starting the day by saying, "I feel healthy! I feel happy! I feel terrific!" He encouraged his employees to do the same. In fact, he encouraged everyone to demonstrate outward enthusiasm and PMA, which stood for a positive mental attitude. His critics thought he was ridiculous, but Mr. Stone got the last laugh, living to age 100, which he had set as his goal, and accumulating hundreds of millions of dollars.

Roswell Crawford is an important character in Ragged Dick and Fame and Fortune because he oozes the world-owes-me-a-living attitude that is so common today. "Roswell was troubled with a large share of pride," Alger writes, "though it might have troubled himself to explain what he had to be proud of."

Roswell never understands the importance of integrity and its relationship to earning one's living. In fact, he once says that he would be happy to be paid $10 a week for nothing. "Well, if I get it, I don't care if I don't earn it," he says. In fact, Roswell is ashamed to be seen in the streets carrying a large bundle as part of a delivery for his job. Before being fired, his boss tells him, "You appear to think yourself of too great consequence to discharge properly the duties of your position."

Contrast that with Richard Hunter's attitude toward his entry-level job when he first starts working at the firm. "I'm ready to do anything that is required of me. I want to make myself useful," he says.

I have the impression that was the same attitude that Horatio Alger had as he approached his goal of becoming a successful writer who could change the world -- or at least the world of the thousands of homeless street urchins in the big city. It is difficult to imagine how bad their plight was. For instance, in 1874, which was seven years after Ragged Dick was first published, there was a little girl named Mary Ellen Wilson, who was beaten unmercifully by her stepmother. She was sent out into the streets ill-clothed in winter. There were other abuses, and they were horrible.

So a social worker named Etta Angel Wheeler wanted to intervene, to help get the child out of that environment. But there were no laws to protect children in such situations. Etta was desperate -- and clever. She enlisted the help of the American Society for the Prevention of Cruelty to Animals because animals were protected by law. Her attorneys argued that Mary Ellen, "as a member of the animal kingdom, deserved the same protection as abused animals." This led to new legislation and various child protective services.

Horatio Alger was at the forefront of this movement. He wanted to help the poor kids in the inner city, and he wound up not only helping them but inspiring millions of other young readers across the country. Many of them transformed their lives as a direct result of the inspiration of the "Stories of Success" that Horatio Alger managed to tell in one exciting setting after another.

It is not surprising that Ernest Hemingway's sister said that her brother could not get enough of Horatio Alger or that Walter Brennan, a famous actor for much of the 20th century, devoured his books. As the legendary Groucho Marx said: "Horatio Alger's books conveyed a powerful message to me and to many of my young friends -- that if you worked hard at your trade, the big chance would eventually come. As a child, I didn't regard it as a myth, and as an old man, I think of it as the story of my life."

Groucho was speaking for millions of Americans in the past and, we hope, millions more in the future.

Rick Newcombe is the founder and CEO of Creators Syndicate, Creators Publishing and Sumner Books.

PREVIEW OF ANOTHER ADVENTURE IN THE HORATIO ALGER "STORIES OF SUCCESS" SERIES

THE YOUNG ADVENTURER

By Horatio Alger, Jr.

"I wish I could pay off the mortgage on my farm," said Mark Nelson soberly, taking his seat on the left of the fireplace, in the room where his wife and family were assembled.

"Have you paid the interest, Mark?" asked his wife.

"Yes. I paid it this afternoon, and it has stripped me of money completely. I have less than five dollars in my pocket toward buying you and the children clothes for the winter."

"Never mind me," said his wife cheerfully. "I am pretty well provided for."

"Why, mother," said Sarah, the oldest daughter, a girl of fourteen, "you haven't had a new dress for a year."

"I have enough to last me till spring, at any rate," said the mother.

"You never buy anything for yourself."

"I don't go in rags, do I?" asked Mrs. Nelson, with a smile.

Mrs. Nelson had a happy disposition, which led her to accept uncomplainingly, and even cheerfully, the sacrifices which, as the wife of a farmer in poor circumstances, she was compelled to make.

"You are right, Sarah," said Mark Nelson. "Your mother never seems to think of herself. She might have been much better off if she had not married me."

The children did not understand this allusion. They had never been told that their mother had received an offer from Squire Hudson, the wealthiest man in the village, but had chosen instead to marry Mark Nelson, whose only property was a small farm, mortgaged for half its value. Her rejected admirer took the refusal hard, for, as much as it was possible for him, he loved the prettiest girl in the village, as Mary Dale was generally regarded. But Mary knew him to be cold and selfish and could not make up her mind to marry him. If she had done so, she would now be living in the finest house in the village, with the chance of spending the winter in New

York or Boston, instead of drudging in a humble home, where there was indeed enough to eat but little money for even necessary purposes. She had never regretted her decision. Her husband, though poor, was generally respected and liked, while the squire, though his money procured him a certain degree of consideration, had no near or attached friends.

To Squire Hudson many in the village paid tribute, for he held mortgages on twenty farms and buildings, and he was strict in exacting prompt payment of the interest semi-annually. It was he to whom Mark Nelson's farm was mortgaged for two thousand dollars. The mortgage had originally been for fifteen hundred dollars, but five years before it had been increased to two thousand, which represented more than half the sum which it would have fetched, if put up for sale. The interest on this sum amounted to a hundred and twenty dollars a year, which Mark Nelson always found it hard to raise. Could he have retained it in his hands and devoted it to the use of his family, it would have helped them wonderfully, with Mrs. Nelson's good management. Tom, the oldest boy, now approaching his sixteenth birthday, looked up from a book he was reading. He was a bright-looking boy, with brown hair, a ruddy complexion and dark-blue eyes, who looked, and was, frank and manly.

"What is the amount of your interest?" he asked.

"Sixty dollars every half-year, Tom. That is what I paid to Squire Hudson this afternoon. It would have made us very comfortable, if I only could have kept it."

"It would have done you more good than the squire," said Sarah.

"He has more money than he knows what to do with," said her father, almost complainingly. "It seems hard that money should be so unevenly distributed."

"Money is not happiness," said Mrs. Nelson quietly.

"No, but it helps to buy happiness."

"I don't think Squire Hudson is as happy a man as you, Mark."

Mark Nelson's face softened as he surveyed his wife and children.

"I am happy at home," he said, "and I don't think the squire is."

"I am sure he isn't," said Tom. "Mrs. Hudson is sour and ill-tempered, and Sinclair -- the only child -- is a second edition of his mother. He is the most unpopular boy in the village."

"Still," said the farmer, not quite convinced, "money is an important element of happiness, and a farmer stands a very poor chance of acquiring it. Tom, I advise you not to be a farmer."

"I don't mean to be if I can help it," said Tom. "I am ready for any opening that offers. I hope some day to pay off the mortgage on the farm and make you a free man, father."

"Thank you for your good intentions, Tom, but two thousand dollars is a large sum of money."

"I know it, father, but I was reading in a daily paper, not long ago, of a boy, as poor as myself, who was worth twenty-five thousand dollars by the time he was thirty. Why shouldn't this happen to me?"

"Don't build castles in the air, Tom," said his mother sensibly.

"At least, mother, I may hope for good luck. I have been wanting to talk to you both about my future prospects. I shall be sixteen next week, and it is time I did something."

"You are doing something -- working on the farm now, Tom."

"That don't count. Father advises me not to be a farmer, and I agree with him. I think I am capable of making my way in the world in some other way, where I can earn more money. There is Walter, who likes the country, to stay with you."

Walter, the third child, was now twelve years of age, with decided country tastes.

"I would like to be a farmer as well as anything," said Walter. "I like the fresh air. I shouldn't like to be cooped up in a store, or to live in the city. Let Tom go if he likes."

"I have no objection," said Mr. Nelson, "but I have neither money nor influence to help him. He will have to make his own way."

"I am not afraid to try," said Tom courageously. "From this day I will look out for a chance, if you and mother are willing."

"I shall not oppose your wishes, Tom," said Mrs. Nelson gravely, "though it will be a sad day for me when you leave your home."

"That isn't the way to look at it, mother," said Tom. "If gold pieces grew on currant bushes, it wouldn't be necessary for me to leave home to make a living."

"I wish they did," said Harry, a boy nine years of age.

"What would you do then, Harry?" asked his brother, smiling.

"I would buy a bicycle and a pair of skates."

"I heard of a boy once who found a penny in the field, right under a potato vine," said Walter.

"I don't believe it," said Harry.

"It's true, for I was the boy."

"Where did it come from?"

"Tom put it there to fool me."

"Won't you put one there to fool me, Tom?" asked Harry.

"You are too smart, Harry," said Tom, laughing. "My pennies are too few to try such experiments. I hope, by the time you are as old as Walter, to give you something better."

The conversation drifted to other topics, with which we are not concerned. Tom, however, did not forget it. He felt that an important question had that evening been decided for him. He had only thought of making a start for himself hitherto. Now he had broached the subject and received the permission of his father and mother. The world was all before him, wherever he chose. His available capital was small, it is true, amounting only to thirty-seven cents and a jack-knife, but he had, besides, a stout heart, a pair of strong hands, an honest face, and plenty of perseverance -- not bad equipment for a young adventurer.